CANADIAN FAMILIES

1900-2000

A BIBLIOGRAPHY

Benjamin Schlesinger, Ph.D., FRSC

Professor Emeritus,
University of Toronto, Faculty of Social Work
and Research Associate,
Robarts Centre for Canadian Studies,
York University

Toronto   *Canadian Scholars' Press*   *2000*

Canadian Families 1900-2000: A Bibliography

Benjamin Schlesinger

First published in 2000 by
Canadian Scholars' Press Inc.
180 Bloor Street West, Suite 1202
Toronto, Ontario
M5S 2V6

Copyright © 2000 Benjamin Schlesinger and Canadian Scholars' Press. All rights reserved. No part of this publication may be photocopied, reproduced, stored in a retrieval system, or transmitted, in any form or by any means, electronic, mechanical or otherwise, without the written permission of Canadian Scholars' Press, except for brief passages quoted for review purposes.

Every reasonable effort has been made to identify copyright holders. CSPI would be pleased to have any errors or omissions brought to its attention.

CSPI acknowledges the financial support of the Government of Canada through the Book Publishing Industry Development Programme for our publishing activities.

Canadian Cataloguing in Publication Data

Schlesinger, Benjamin, 1928-
    Canadian families 1900-2000 : a bibliography

Includes bibliographical references.
ISBN 1-55130-155-5

1. Family – Canada – Bibliography. I. Title.

Z5118.F2S283 2000   016.30685'0971   C00-931752-X

Managing Editor: Ruth Bradley-St-Cyr
Marketing Manager: Susan Cuk
Cover design: Amy Seagram

00 01 02 03 04 05 06   6 5 4 3 2 1

Printed and bound in Canada by Brown Book Company

"To my way of thinking, the best and surest way of developing generous and idealistic hearts, of giving the community men and women who are well-balanced and conscious of their responsibilities to their country, is to protect the family, for the family — far from opposing the interests of society — is capable of giving to the universe the human beings who are prepared to put justice and truth before their own personal interests."

Governor General Georges Vanier
Opening Speech, The Canadian Conference
on the Family, June 7, 1964.

PREFACE

This bibliography is an attempt to list most of the English entries related to Canadian families, covering the 1900-1999 period. In our search, we may have missed some items, and we apologize for this omission.

The 943 entries have been categorized under topical headings. Some of the citations are annotated. We have added an author index to facilitate the reader, to find specific references.

An introductory essay highlights some of the important occasions and research findings related to Canadian families during the 20th century. We have ordered the highlights in chronological order.

Special thanks to Angela Umbrello, who typed the manuscript, and put it into the existing format. Dr. Robert Glossop of the Vanier Institute of the Family gave helpful suggestions for entries to the bibliography.

We dedicate this publication to all of Canada's families. May the 21st century bring them health and happiness.

Benjamin Schlesinger

CONTENTS

Canadian Families: Personal Glimpses 1

Bibliography:
    Adoption 12
    Bibliographies/References 13
    Canadian Society and Families 15
    Children and Youth 15
    Child Care 17
    Childlessness 18
    Cohabitation 20
    Collected Readings on Family Life 21
    Data Base Related to Families 22
    Demographic Trends 23
    Divorce:
        Custody 27
        Mediation 29
        Overview 29
    Economics and Family Life 31
    Ethnic Family Life 33
    Family Caregiving 40
    Family Life: Overview 41
    Family Models 45
    Family: Social Services 45
    Farm Families 46
    Fathers 47
    Fertility and Family Life 48
    French-Canadian Families 49
    Gay and Lesbian Families 50
    Gender and Family 52
    Grandparents 52
    Historical Family Research 53
    Housewives/Housework 57
    Housing and Family Life 58
    Intermarriage 59
    Kinship 60
    Legal Aspects Related to Families 61
    Marriage 63
    Mental Health and Family Life 66
    Military/Foreign Service and Family Life 67
    Non-Traditional Families 68

One Parent Families:
- Overview 68
  - Non-Married Parents 71
  - Separation 72
  - Widows/Widowers 73
- Postponed Parenthood 74
- Poverty and Family Life 75
- Remarriage/Stepfamilies 75
- Reproductive Technologies and Family Life 79
- Sandwich Generation and Boomerang Offspring 79
- Seniors 81
- Sexual Issues in Family Life 84
- Singlehood 85
- Social Policy and the Family 86
- Strengths of Families 88
- Women and Family Life:
  - Overview 89
  - Work and Family 90
- Women: Societal Issues 91
- Related Topics:
  - Family Issues 93
  - Family Research 95
  - Family Surveys 95
  - Population Studies 96
  - Source Books 97

About the Author 99
Author Index 100
Websites Related to Canadian Families 119
Resources Related to Canadian Families 120

CANADIAN FAMILIES: PERSONAL GLIMPSES

I have been participating in examining Canadian families since 1960, a period of 40 years.
I have chosen to highlight in this personal discussion, some of the important documents that focused on Canadian family life. They come from the 1964-1994 period, and include some historical trends.

WHAT'S PAST IS PROLOGUE

One of the most useful summaries of Canadian family history has been published by Nett (1981). She points out that by 1977, only nine Canadian entries could be found in a guide to the literature on the family in history (Milden, 1977). Nett (1981: 242-255) has gathered the following Canadian historical trends related to Canadian families.

- The transition of the family from both a production and a consumption unit to primarily a consumption unit.

- In the colonial period, the family's activities were still home-centered and each member of the household, including grandparents, had tasks to perform which were vital to the maintenance of the family.

- The type of household in which most Canadians resided, from the time of settlement in Acadia, New France, New England and later Upper Canada, was the nuclear, or "simple" family household. This was the case regardless of geographical locale or whether the residences were backwoods, settled farm, village, or urban.

- Although the situation in families in Quebec and Upper Canada must have stabilized substantially after 1769, life expectancy was still sufficiently short at the age of marriage that three generations living under one roof was a possibility for only the most favoured families, and then for no longer than a few years

- Marriage was a necessity for both women and men in the early years of the fur trade and settlement, and was considered desirable even after the political and economic situation had stabilized, is attested to by the marriage and remarriage rates. In both French and English colonies almost all young people married, and in New France a high proportion remarried. The persistent shortage of women and the pressures to populate the colonies kept the marriage rates high until at least the 1880s, with the decline in Quebec at this time associated with the developing scarcity of land.

- Over the life cycle of the average family there were brief periods when a newly married couple lived with the parents of one of the spouses, or when an elderly couple or parent shared the home of a married child. Indeed, among both English and French Canadians in rural Ontario, marriage was dependent upon the ability of a couple to establish a separate household.

- Studies of families in the early years suggest that children were involved in family and society in much the same way as their parents. This may account for so few observations about them in accounts of life prior to the middle of the nineteenth century.

- Children in earlier times were an important source of labour, both in rural Canada and in the cities during industrialization. Compulsory school attendance and the provision of other social welfare facilities in the last part of the nineteenth century changed that situation.

- Families settling in Eastern Ontario as late as the mid-nineteenth century, produced their own food, yarn, fabric, clothing, rugs, and crops. Since the participation of women and children was crucial in survival, the farm economies were indeed family economies.

For updates on these findings, see the section on Historical Aspects of the Family in this bibliography.

THE CANADIAN CONFERENCE ON THE FAMILY, JUNE 7-19, 1964

The Canadian Conference on the Family was founded by Their Excellencies the Governor-General and Madame Vanier. Here is how His Excellency explained the growth of the idea:

> During the past 35 years, as we moved about various parts of this and other countries of the Atlantic Community, both my wife and I have been impressed frequently and forcefully by the vital importance of family life. Meeting and talking with people of all conditions, we have witnessed the inner strength and confidence of those nurtured in the love of a true family, and we have observed the lonely hopelessness and moral difficulty of those deprived of the support that only a family can provide. Bearing this in mind, my wife and I are anxious to see established in our native land an enduring association of many professions dedicated to the reinforcement of family living.

> From the beginning the Conference officers sought, within the time limits, to involve as many people as possible in order to awaken a new recognition of the importance of family life and to make the Conference representative of the whole country. Mainly through the resourcefulness of Conference information officers with the aid of the press and other media, Canadians followed the Conference developments with interest. In the early months of 1964 organizations and individuals submitted 71 reports, briefs and papers which formed part of the resource material placed before the Conference. Finally, some 350 persons accepted invitations to attend, which was the number that space permitted.

> However the principal task of the year was that of program planning. The immediate need was to assemble all of the present knowledge of Canadian families and at the same time to discover the points on which information was lacking. Dr. Frederick Elkin was invited to meet this need and his findings were published in a book entitled *The Family in*

Canada. Three major responsibilities remained. First the broad topics for principal papers were selected and their authors chosen. Secondly, on the basis of consultations across the country, some twenty specific subjects were identified for small round-table discussion. Thirdly, a Youth Evening was planned for the second day of the Conference.

On June 7, 1964, there assembled in the gardens of Rideau Hall a group of 1500 Canadians. The first Canadian Conference on the Family was ready to begin. Lillian Thomson was the Executive Director of the Conference.

THE FAMILY IN CANADA BY FREDERICK ELKIN, 1964

Professor Elkin, Chairman of the Department of Sociology, York University was asked by the Canadian Conference on the Family to produce a volume of present knowledge and gaps about Canadian families. Elkin (1964: 10) states:

> We present a report on our knowledge and research on the Canadian family. Occasionally, to give perspective or more depth, certain extraneous materials such as demographic data, researches conducted outside of Canada, and commentaries, especially by Canadian scholars, are included. The report does not presume to be exhaustive; limits of time especially prevented us from searching out all the pertinent material.

At the conclusion of his report, Elkin (176) pointed out that:

> The family in Canada has a western heritage and has moved with western society. Many of the problems and trends noted — the changing roles of women, the multi-problem family, the wife working for pay, the persisting but changing form of kinship ties, the convergence between socio-economic levels of family size and child rearing patterns, the increasing freedom of individuals to choose and depart from their mates, the increasing conscious control of family size, the decreasing importance of family units in large business operations — are no different in Canada than in other parts of the world.

He noted however some of Canada's unique situation when he stated (176):

> Canada also has its unique problems and characteristics. We have a lower proportion of wives working for pay and a lower divorce rate than most western industrialized countries. Our weather creates distinctive problems of seasonal employment and limits the areas of settlement for retired people. Our mosaic of ethnic groups has no direct counterpart anywhere in the world. Our history links us especially with the cultures of England and France and our geography to the culture of the United States. We have above all a French Canada with its unique historical development for 400 years. And all this has its effect on the institutions, value systems and sentimental identifications which have been incorporated into our way of thought and life.

His two major suggestions for further action included the following two ideas (180):

1. That a national clearing house for family studies be established with the purpose of bringing together and organizing the many scattered studies and researches that have been conducted on the family in Canada. Such a clearing house could serve as a guide to active workers and researchers and a communication link between those interested parties who are of different languages or geographically distant.

2. That a research advisory centre on the family be established to assist any group or student seriously interested in conducting research on the family in Canada. The centre would be available for consultation in setting up and carrying out any research that might contribute to our knowledge of the family. Perhaps too the centre might be in a position to encourage publication of deserving works.

THE VANIER INSTITUTE OF THE FAMILY: 1965

The Institute was established in 1965 under the patronage of the late Governor General and Madame Vanier in response to a need recognized at the first Canadian Conference on the Family.

The Vanier Institute of the Family has one essential purpose: to strengthen family life in Canada and to help families adapt to our rapidly changing society. The Institute regards the family as a dynamic and changing institution and recognizes the interdependence of the individual, the family and society. Its resolve is to remain flexible and responsive to the needs of the family and to the pressures on family life. The Institute is concerned with the quality of life of Canadian families of all types. It cooperates with and works through social and educational agencies that are in direct contact with families.

The Institute's membership represents the various ethnic, social, religious, occupational, and geographical elements of Canadian society.

The Work of the Institute

The program of the Vanier Institute of the Family focuses on research, communication and education, and social action. The Institute does its work by gathering information about the family, by stimulating research into aspects of the family of which little is known, and by informing Canadians of those things that tend to strengthen the family and improve the quality of family life. The Institute provides a forum, across Canada, for all groups concerned with the family. It conducts seminars and consultations on family problems and programs that bring together for discussion the leaders in a variety of professions and fields of interest, including health, education, law, social welfare, town planning, religion, sociology, economics, demography, industry, labour, youth and parents. Whenever appropriate, the Institute endeavours to influence public policy to ensure consideration of the effects of such policy on families.

The publication *Transition* is published quarterly by the Institute, and contains Canadian family content.

THE INVENTORY: CANADIAN FAMILY RESEARCH AND STUDIES — JOHN SPENCER, 1967

Professor John Spencer, of the Faculty of Social Work, University of Toronto produced an inventory of Canadian family studies (Spencer, 1967). In his summary of the existing studies he found the following trends.

1. The most striking weakness in contemporary research on the family in Canada is the lack of broadly based studies of structure and function, of roles and relationships, and of occupation, income and expenditure. The lack of large-scale researches based on theoretical foundations is especially noticeable.

2. We are in need of comparative studies which are able to do justice to the rich variety of characteristics of families across Canada. Cross-cultural research of this kind might usefully be related to family research in other countries. For it is on research of this kind that theories will be tested and revised and new knowledge of family life will become available.

3. Although Canada possesses an invaluable source of competently organized statistical data on different aspects of the family, on population, census data, vital statistics, mobility, income and expenditure and so forth, through the publications of the Dominion Bureau of Statistics, must still remains to be done. There are, for example, the opportunities for secondary analysis through which scholars can dig more deeply into those statistics which already exist. A case in point would be the analysis of tax statistics relating the impact of different forms of taxation to different patterns of family expenditure in different types of family.

4. What is lacking is research which examines the changes in role structure and family relationships, the division of labour and authority and the changes in family budgeting and in child-rearing in relation to this general trend. Also absent from the inventory are reports of studies which focus on the question of employment and the possible reorganization of hours and work-shifts in order to take account of family responsibilities.

5. The inventory provides evidence of the growing interest in the family on the part of many different disciplines and professions. The family certainly is not, and never has been, the prerogative of a single discipline or of a single profession. The studies listed here are a reflection of its importance to lawyers, doctors, architects, town planners, agriculturalists, economists, home economists, educators, social workers, doctors, psychologists and the clergy, as well as to many others. But perhaps most important of all there is in these studies a reflection of its meaning to the ordinary parent and citizen.

   He also commented on the importance of Canadian family research and family policy in Canada (xii):

The idea of a family-centred social policy is easy to state but the principles on which it might rest or the precise forms which it could take are not easy to formulate. They raise complex questions of sociology, psychology, economics and law, to mention only four of the major disciplines involved. One of the purposes of research, therefore, is to lay the ground-work of knowledge on which policy formulation may be based. This inventory provides at least a rough guide to the areas where current studies are going on and above all gives us some indication of the gaps.

THE REPORT OF THE ROYAL COMMISSION ON THE STATUS OF WOMEN, 1970

On February 3, 1967, the government of Canada announced the formation of a Royal Commission on the Status of Women. The purpose of the inquiry, as set out by the cabinet, was to recommend what steps might be taken by the federal government to ensure for women equal opportunities with men in all aspects of Canadian society. On December 11, 1970, the final report was released.

The commission, on their cross-Canada trips, received 468 submissions from individuals and organizations, and 890 witnesses appeared before them. Thirty-five special studies were prepared for the commission ranging from Women and the Criminal Law to Daycare. Sixty-five specialists and experts helped in discussions, consultations, and correspondence. The 488 page report makes 167 recommendations. Some of the highlights of this report were in the following areas.

Marriage
No one in Canada could marry until age eighteen if a recommendation of the Royal Commission on the Status of Women is implemented.

The commission asks the federal government to pass a law making the minimum age for marriage eighteen for both men and women.

Commissioners admit that eighteen is "an arbitrary figure" but note that the legal age for marriage in Canada now ranges from twelve (for girls in Québec) to 21 (in six provinces).

"No exceptions at all should be made in order to permit a marriage when one or both parties have not reached the age of eighteen," the commission stated.

Daycare
A $500 million network of daycare centres in Canada is envisioned by the Royal Commission on the Status of Women.

The commission estimates that would be the annual cost of caring for 450,0000 children under six years of age who will need daycare within the next few years.

It asks that the federal government pay half the operating costs of the centres and, for seven years, 70 per cent of the capital cost.

The commission asks, too, that loans for building and removing buildings for daycare centres be available under the National Housing Act and that housing developers be allowed to include space for centres when applying for NHA building loans.

Sex Education and Information
Adequate knowledge of the body's reproductive function and of human sexual behaviour should be taught at primary and secondary schools.

It recommends that adult men and women should be able to get birth control information and also that young girls be informed and given access to contraceptives.

"Since many teenagers do have sexual intercourse, they also need the means to avoid conception and should therefore receive appropriate advice and have access to the most effective birth control information and advice," the report says.

It also asks provincial health departments to organize family planning clinics, including mobile ones for remote areas.

Women and Work
Mandatory maternity leave, equal minimum wage rates in provinces where separate minimums apply to men and women, bringing paid household employees under minimum wage protection, and a whole series of changes to open more opportunities to women were proposed.

The report says that Canadian legislation has failed to win equality for women in economic life and blames unions and employers for the establishment and continuance of different pay scales for women workers.

Recent federal statistics show that in 1968, Canadian men were earning an average $6,779 a year, while female workers averaged only $3,984.

THE SOCIAL SCIENCES AND HUMANITIES RESEARCH COUNCIL: FAMILY STUDIES (1978-1993)

Since its inception in 1978, the Social Sciences and Humanities Research Council of Canada has supported hundreds of research projects that examine ongoing or newly emerging issues and problems related to the family. A booklet lists close to 475 of those projects, which cover a vast range of subjects from the social and economic dimensions of family life to the religious, cultural, educational and historical experiences of families in Canadian society and throughout the world.

Published in commemoration of the 1994 International Year of the Family, this document is a reference source for anyone interested in research related especially to family life and family issues.

It is of interest that during the 1997-1998 grants given by SSHRC, four projects were funded in the family area out of 47 grants given in the area of sociology.

TABLE ONE
SELECTED FAMILY STUDIES IN CANADA SPONSORED BY THE SSHRC* - 1978-1993
TOPICS

• Adoption Resources	• Fatherhood
• Changing Family and Children	• Grandparenthood
• Daycare	• Latchkey Families
• Death and Family Life	• Marriage
• Divorce	• Mid-Life Families
• Ethnic Families	• Multi-Problem Families
• Family Demography	• One-Parent Families
• History of the Family	• Post-Modern Families
• Family and Poverty	• Postponed Parenthood
• Family Histories	• Remarriage/Step-parenting
• Family Life of Seniors	• Shared Parenting
• Farm Families	• Two-earner Families

*Source: Social Sciences and Humanities Research Council (1994) *Canadian Research on Family Issues*. Ottawa: SSHRC.

THE INTERNATIONAL YEAR OF THE FAMILY — 1994

During 1994, the Angus Reid Group conducted a survey of 21,051 adults nation wide to find out the *state of the family in Canada*. Some of the findings indicate the changes among Canadian families in the 1990s.

- Nearly two out of every ten adult Canadians (17%) have been divorced. Of these, one third (35%) are either remarried or living common-law with a new partner. Eleven percent of Canadian adults are divorced or separated and living without a partner.

- Most parents (84%) say they are satisfied with the amount of time they spend with their children, and nearly half (45%) say they are very satisfied. Respondents who work half-time or less at paid employment are more likely to report being "very satisfied" with the time they spend with their children (49%) compared to those who work more than 40 hours per week (32%).

- Parents say they spend an average of 6.3 hours per week watching television with their children and just one-third that amount of time (2.1 hours) on helping them with homework. Youth in the survey reported that they watch TV on their own for 8.6 hours per week. Nearly nine out of ten families (85%) eat dinner together as a family more than three times per week.

- Four in ten parents (40%) say they would quit the labour force to stay home with their children if they could afford it. At the same time, nearly half of parents working full-time (46%) and six in ten parents working part-time (61%) say they have a good balance between their jobs and time with their families. One parent in eight (13%) reports feeling very guilty about work time they spend away from their children. For parents of children under the age of twelve, the number rises to nearly one in five (18%).

- There is strong support for government-supported elder care (85% overall) and a national child care program (75%). Four in ten Canadians (40%) support family benefits for same-sex couples.

- One out of ten Canadian adults (11%) is responsible for caring for a family member other than a spouse or child, most commonly their mothers (34%) or mothers-in-law (22%).

- Women (14%) were twice as likely as men (7%) to feel their spouses' work requirements have limited their own careers. One in five working women (21%) reported that "their gender" has limited their job advancement compared to 8% of men.

- Approval of family benefits for same-sex couples and of same-sex couples raising children is generally stronger among younger groups, among women, and in central Canada, especially Quebec. For example, four in ten (40%) of the younger generation believe that same-sex couples raising children is acceptable, compared with 27% of the general population.

LOOKING AHEAD TO THE 21st CENTURY

It is extremely difficult to make predictions of the family. In examining the Canadian literature related to families, I have looked into the crystal ball and predict some of the following trends in the 21st century:

- We will have fewer marriages

- More Canadians will marry in their 30s

- Fewer children will be born, and they will be born mostly when their parents are in their 30s and early 40s

- We will have more daycare services available for children

- The role of the father will change and become more egalitarian

- We will have more inter-ethnic marriages

- Cohabitation (living together) will increase

- We will have fewer divorces, thus fewer remarriages

- Dual working couples will increase

- More married women will be in the labour force

- Fewer women will be full-time unpaid homemakers

- We will have more seniors (age 65+) and fewer family caregivers for this age cohort

- All levels of government will have to re-examine existing family programs such as pensions, unemployment insurance, health insurance, welfare allowances, etc. A "ministry for the family" will be instituted on the federal level

- We will accept gay and lesbian parenthood and family life

- More grandparents will be raising grandchildren

- We will have more "single mothers by choice" in their 30s

- Our lifespan will increase.

I leave the last word to John Peters, of Wilfrid Laurier University (Peters, 1995: 78) in Waterloo, Ontario:

> On the societal level the institution of the family serves an important function. It is the largest social service industry in the world. It serves as caregiver to the young and dependent, the ill, the aged and the healthy person. In most cases the family gives social support and encouragement to its members. Our society expects parents to provide the economic necessities of life for their children. The state expects children to be socialized by parents in democracy, in respect for the law, and the rights of others. Parents are obligated to cooperate in facilitating children to become literate. The relationships between the family and the state will not diminish.

BIBLIOGRAPHY

ADOPTION

1. Cohen, J.S. and Westhues, A. (1987–1988). **Healthy Functioning Families for Adoptive and Foster Children.** Toronto: Faculty of Social Work, University of Toronto (2 volumes). This two-volume study examines long-term foster care and adoption of special-needs children.

2. Daly, K. and Sobol, M. (1993). **Adoption in Canada: Final Report.** Ottawa: Health and Welfare Canada.

3. Daly, K.J. and Sobol, M.P. (1992). **Adoption as an Alternative for Infertile Couples: Prospects and Trends.** No. 210E. Ottawa: Royal Commission on New Reproductive Technologies.

4. Garber, R. (1985). **Disclosure of Adoption Information**. Toronto: Ministry of Community and Social Services, Ontario. A review of adoption disclosure in various countries, and recommendations for Ontario.

5. Hepworth, H.P. (1980). **Foster Care and Adoption in Canada**. Ottawa: Canadian Council Social Development. A discussion of the child welfare services during the last twenty years (1960–1977). The focus is on foster care and adoption.

6. Kirk, H. (1964). **Shared Fate.** New York: Free Press. A study of adoption related to Canadian society.

7. Kirk, H. (1981). **Adoptive Kinship: A Modern Institution In Need of Reform**. Toronto: Butterworths, 1981. A discussion of adoption, including a comprehensive review of the literature.

8. Langlois, R.J. (1981). **A Different Understanding: Adoption.** Toronto: TV Ontario. This booklet discusses the adoption experience.

9. Lipman, M. (1984). **Adoption in Canada: Two Decades in Review.** In *Adoption: Current Issues and Trends,* edited by P. Sachdev. Toronto: Butterworths.

10. March, K. (1995). **The Stranger Who Bore Me: Adoptee–Birth Mother Relationships.** Toronto: University of Toronto Press. Sixty reunited adoptees in Canada discuss their journeys in finding their birth mother.

11. Marcus, C. (1981). **Who is my Mother?** Toronto: Macmillan of Canada. The voices of the real people who make up the adoption triangle. Birth parents, adoptive parents, and adoptees talk about their lives.

12. Ministry of Community and Social Services (1986). **How to Adopt in Ontario.** Toronto. This booklet describes how adoption takes place in Ontario.

13. Ministry of Community and Social Services (1986). **Ontario's New Adoption Disclosure Policy.** Toronto. The new open approach to adoption disclosure in Ontario is reviewed in this document.

14. Redmond, W. and Sleighholm, S. (1982). **Once Removed: Voices from Inside the Adoption Triangle.** Toronto: McGraw Hill-Ryerson. Case histories of persons involved in adoption.

15. Sachdev, P., ed. (1984). **Adoption: Current Issues and Trends.** Toronto: Butterworths. Various articles discuss adoption in Canada.

16. Schlesinger, B. (1978). **Adoption Disclosure: Controversy and Consensus.** *Australian Social Welfare,* 8, pp. 35-37.

17. Sobol, M. and Daly, K. (1995). **Adoptive Practices in Canada: Emerging Trends and Challenges.** *Child Welfare,* 74, pp. 655-678.

18. Vanier Institute of the Family (1992). **Adoption in Canada: A Profile.** *Transition,* pp. 4-5.

19. Webber, M. (1998). **As If Kids Mattered: What's Wrong in the World of Child Protection and Adoption.** Toronto: Key Porter Books.

BIBLIOGRAPHIES/REFERENCES

20. Ackerman, R.J. (1987). **Children of Alcoholics: A Bibliography and Resource Guide.** Toronto: Addiction Research Foundation. Contains more than 700 references related to Canadian and American literature.

21. Gregorovich, A., ed. (1972). **Canadian Ethnic Groups Bibliography.** Toronto: Ontario Department of the Provincial Secretary and Citizenship.

22. Hawley, D. L., (compiler) (1985). **Women and Aging: A Comprehensive Bibliography.** Burnaby, B.C.: Simon Fraser University, The Gerontology Research Centres. Contains items on family issues related to the topic. Not annotated.

23. Health and Welfare Canada (1985). **Mediation and Divorce: A Bibliography.** Ottawa. This bibliography contains 368 items related to divorce and mediation in Canada and the United States.

24. Lebevre, M. (1987). **Selected Bibliography (1975–1985) on Pastoral Reflection and Action about the Family.** *Pastoral Sciences*, 6, pp. 185-226. (Saint Paul University). A comprehensive annotated bibliography on pastoral counselling and family life.

25. Mazur, C. and Pepper, S. (1984). **Women in Canada: A Bibliography 1965 to 1982.** Toronto: Ontario Institute for Studies in Education. Includes items related to aging, daycare, divorce and other related topics to the family.

26. McPherson, K. (1983). **A Round the Clock Job: A Selected Bibliography on Women's Work at Home in Canada.** Ottawa: Social Sciences and Humanities Research Council of Canada. The bibliography contains items from the 1845–1982 period.

27. Schlesinger, B. (2000). **Jewish Families: A Bibliography.** Toronto: Canadian Scholar's Press. Fully annotated bibliography of various aspects of Jewish families.

28. Schlesinger, B. (1987). **Jewish Family Issues: A Resource Guide.** New York: Garland Press. A guide to understanding Jewish family life that contains three essays and an annotated bibliography of 524 items.

29. Schlesinger, B., ed. (1985). **The One–Parent Family in the 1980s.** Toronto: University of Toronto Press. Five essays discuss Canadian one-parent families. The 490 bibliographic items include American and Canadian sources.

30. Schlesinger, B. (1983). **Remarriage: A Review and Annotated Bibliography.** Chicago: Council of Planning Librarians. A review of the literature on remarriage in Canada and the United States, and an annotated bibliography up to 1983.

31. Schlesinger, B. (1978). **The One–Parent Family: Perspectives and Annotated Bibliography.** Toronto: University of Toronto Press. Seven hundred and fifty annotations cover Canadian and American items related to one-parent families.

32. Schlesinger, B. and Schlesinger, R. (1989). **Canadian Families: A Resource Guide.** Toronto: OISE Press.

33. Schlesinger, B. and Schlesinger, R., eds. (1988). **Abuse of the Elderly: Issues and Annotated Bibliography.** Toronto: University of Toronto Press. Nine papers discuss elder abuse in Canada. The 267 item bibliography contains Canadian and American references.

34. Spence, A. (compiler) (1979). **Homosexuality in Canada: A Bibliography.** Toronto: Pink Triangle Press. A bibliography of Canadian writings on homosexuality including psychology and sociology, up to 1978.

CANADIAN SOCIETY AND FAMILIES

35. Adams, M. (1997). **Sex in the Snow: Canadian Social Values at the End of the Millennium.** Toronto: Viking (Penguin). This book is about the changing characteristics of Canadians. Includes a discussion of seniors, boomers, the generation X and women and men.

36. Angus Reid Group (1994). **The State of the Family in Canada.** Ottawa. A public research study on Canadians' attitudes and opinions about issues facing families in Canada today.

37. Bibby, R.G. (1995). **The Bibby Report: Social Trends Canadian Style.** Toronto: Stoddart Publishing. A survey of Canadians related to varied aspects of life including marriage.

38. Foot, D.K. and Stoffman, D. (1996). **Boom, Bust and Echo.** Toronto: Macfarlane Walter & Ross. A demographic view of population changes in Canada, including the Sandwich Generation. If we understand changing demographics, we can understand changing family patterns.

39. Owram, D. (1996). **Born at the Right Time: A History of the Baby Boom Generation.** Toronto: University of Toronto Press. Canada's baby boomers will also move into the Sandwich Generation. A fascinating historical look at this cohort from the end of the Second World War to the close of the 1960s.

CHILDREN AND YOUTH

40. Alberta Committee on Children and Youth (1982). **What you should know about Alberta Children and their Families: The Darker Side.** Edmonton. This book attempts to raise the awareness of Albertans to the needs of Alberta's children and families.

41. Ambert, A.M. (1992). **The Effect of Children on Parents.** New York: Haworth Press. A Canadian sociologist examines the research literature related to children and parents.

42. Ambert, A.M. and Saucier, J.F. (1984). **Adolescents' Academic Success and Aspirations by Parental Marital Status.** *Canadian Review of Sociology and Anthropology,* 21 (1), pp. 62-74.

43. Bala, N. (1991). **An Introduction to Child Protection Problems.** In *Canadian Child Welfare Law: Children, Families and the State,* edited by N. Bala, J.P. Hornick and R. Vogl. Toronto: Thompson Educational Publishing.

44. Barnes, G.E., Greenwood, L. and Sommer, R. (1991). **Courtship Violence in a Canadian Sample of Male College Students.** *Family Relations,* 40, pp. 37-44.

45. Bibby, R.W. and Posterski, D.C. (1985). **The Emerging Generation: An Inside Look at Canada's Teenagers.** Toronto: Irwin Publishing.

46. Breton, R. (1972). **Social and Academic Factors in the Career Decisions of Canadian Youth.** Ottawa: Information Canada.

47. Burke, M.A., Crompton, S., Jones, A. and Nessner, K. (1991). **Caring for Children.** *Canadian Social Trends,* pp. 12-15.

48. Cregheur, A. and Devereaux, M.S. (1991). **Canada's Children.** *Canadian Social Trends,* pp. 2-5.

49. Douthitt, R.A. and Fedy, K.J. (1990). **The Cost of Raising Children in Canada.** Toronto: Butterworths. The data for this study was taken from Statistics Canada's 1982 Family Expenditure survey.

50. Ellis, D. and Sayer, L. (1986). **When I Grow Up: Career Expectations and Aspirations of Canadian School Children.** Ottawa: Labour Canada. The findings of a study of 700 children aged 6–14 years of age.

51. Greene, B. (1991). **Canada's Children: Investing in Our Future.** Ottawa: Supply and Services Canada.

52. Hébert, J. (1986). **Youth: A Plan of Action.** Ottawa: Senate of Canada. A report on the needs of Canada's young people.

53. Hobart, C.W. (1991). **Interest in Parenting at the End of the Eighties: A Study of Canadian Students.** *Canadian Studies in Population,* 18, pp. 75-100.

54. Hobart, C.W. (1981). **Sources of Egalitarianism in Young Unmarried Canadians.** The *Canadian Journal of Sociology,* 6, pp. 261-282. This article analyses changes between 1967–77 in marital role egalitarianism among randomly selected samples of anglophone and francophone male and female post-secondary students.

55. Hobart, C.W. (1973). **Attitudes Toward Parenthood Among Canadian Young People.** *Journal of Marriage and the Family,* 35 (1), pp. 71-82.

56. Newman, F. (1988). **Children and Death.** Federation of Women Teacher's Association of Ontario Newsletter, 6, pp. 26-30. Toronto: Federation of Women Teachers Association of Ontario. A discussion of how death affects children.

57. Peters, J.F. (1987). **Youth, Family and Employment.** *Adolescence,* 22, pp. 465-473.

58. Ravaneka, Z.R., Rajulton, F. and Burch, T.K. (1995). **A Cohort analysis of home-leaving in Canada.** *Journal of Comparative Family Studies,* 26, pp. 179-194.

59. Saucier, J.F. and Ambert, A.M. (1983). **Parental Marital Status and Adolescents' Optimism About Their Future.** *Journal of Youth and Adolescence,* 11, pp. 345-354.

60. Scott, K., Director (1996). **The Progress of Canada's Children 1996.** Ottawa: Canadian Council on Social Development. This document examines some of the major issues related to children and their families. Demographic analysis is used to highlight areas of need in Canada.

61. Smith, N.F. and Grenier, M.K. (1975). **English and French Canadian Children's Views of Parents.** *Canadian Journal of Behavioural Science,* 7, pp. 40-53.

62. Wargon, S.T. (1979). **Children in Canadian Families.** Ottawa: Statistics Canada.

CHILD CARE

63. Canadian Advisory Council on the Status of Women (1986). **Report of the Task Force of Child Care.** Ottawa: Minister of Supply and Services.

64. Cooke, K. (1986). **Report on the Task Force on Child Care.** Ottawa: Minister of Supply and Services. A comprehensive review of child care in Canada including present needs.

65. Denholm, C., Ferguson, R. and Pence, A., eds. (1987). **Professional Child and Youth Care: The Canadian Perspective.** Vancouver: The University of British Columbia Press. An analysis of professional child care in Canada. Also presents an overview of child care.

66. Friendly, M. and Rothman, L. (1995). **Miles To Go: The Policy Context of Child Care in Canada.** *Child Welfare,* 74, pp. 503-524.

67. Johnson, L.C. and Dineen, J. (1981). **The Kid Trade: The Daycare Crisis in Canada.** Toronto: McGraw Hill-Ryerson, 1981. Explores the private homes that offer daycare for children in Canada.

68. Krashinsky, M. (1987). **The Cooke Report on Child Care: A Critique.** *Canadian Public Policy,* 13, pp. 294-303. An examination of the costs involved in implementing a full policy of full subsidies to daycare in Canada, available to all working parents.

69. Lero, D., Goelman, H., Pence, A., Brockman, L. and Nuttall, S. (1992). **Canadian National Child Care Study: Parental Work Patterns and Child Care Needs.** Catalogue 89-529. Ottawa: Minister of Supply and Services.

70. Lero, D.S. (1993). **In Transition: Changing Patterns of Work, Family Life, and Child Care.** *Transition,* 23, pp. 5-7.

71. Lero, D.S. and Kyle, I. (1991). **Work, Families and Child Care in Ontario.** In *Children, Families and Public Policy in the 1990s,* edited by L.C. Johnson and D. Barnhorst, pp. 25-72. Toronto: Thompson Educational Publishing.

72. Lero, D.S., Pence, A.R., Shields, M., Brockman, L.M. and Goelman, H. (1992). **Canadian National Child Care Study: Introductory Report.** Catalogue 89-526E. Ottawa: Statistics Canada.

73. National Council of Welfare (1988). **Child Care: A Better Alternative.** Ottawa.

74. Pence, A.R., ed. (1992). **Canadian National Child Care Study: Canadian Child Care in Context — Perspectives from the Provinces and Territories.** Ottawa: Statistics Canada, Health and Welfare Canada.

CHILDLESSNESS

75. Grindstaff, C.F., Balakrishnan, T.R. and Ebanks, G.E. (1981). **Socio–demographic Correlates of Childlessness: An Analysis of the 1971 Canadian Census.** The *Canadian Journal of Sociology,* 6, pp. 337-351. This study utilized 1971 Canada census data. The individual files of women who were ever married or currently married, over fifteen years of age, and childless were investigated.

76. Matthews, R. and Martin-Matthews, A. (1986). **Infertility and Involuntary Childlessness: The Transition to Nonparenthood.** *Journal of Marriage and the Family,* 48, pp. 641-649.

77. Ramu, G.N. (1985). **Voluntarily Childless and Parental Couples: A Comparison of their Lifestyle Characteristics.** *Life Styles: A Journal of Changing Patterns,* 7, pp. 130-145.

78. Ramu, G.N. (1984). **Family Background and Perceived Marital Happiness: A Comparison of Voluntary Childless Couples and Parents.** The *Canadian*

Journal of Sociology, 9, pp. 47-68. A study in Winnipeg of voluntary childless couples.

79. Ramu, G.N. and Tavuchis, N. (1986). **The Valuation of Children and Parenthood Among the Voluntary Childless and Parental Couples in Canada.** *Journal of Comparative Family Studies,* 17, pp. 99-116. A non-random sample of couples is studied to examine the values that influence fertility decisions.

80. Rao, K.V. (1987). **Childlessness in Ontario and Quebec: Results from 1971 and 1981 Census Data.** *Canadian Studies in Population,* 14, pp. 27-46.

81. Rao, K.V. and Balakrishnan, T.R. (1988). **Recent Trends and Sociodemographic Covariates of Childlessness in Canada.** *Canadian Studies in Population,* 15, pp. 181-200.

82. Rempel, J. (1985). **Childless Elderly: What Are They Missing?** *Journal of Marriage and the Family,* 47, pp. 343-348. Using Canadian statistics, the author shows that the childless elderly are more financially secure and in better health.

83. Tomes, N. (1985). **Childlessness in Canada 1971: A Further Analysis.** The *Canadian Journal of Sociology,* 10, pp. 37-68. A statistical analysis of childlessness in 1971.

84. Veevers, J.E. (1980). **Childless By Choice.** Toronto: Butterworths. This book is concerned with the lives of "unusual" couples who decided not to have children. The purpose of the book is to report on some of the causes and consequences of being childless by choice.

85. Veevers, J.E. (1979). **Voluntary Childlessness: A Review of Issues and Evidence.** *Marriage and Family Review,* 2, pp. 1-26. The author reviews her own Canadian studies on voluntary childlessness and the American studies.

86. Veevers, J.E. (1973). **Voluntary Childless Wives: An Exploratory Study.** *Sociology and Social Research,* 57, pp. 346-366.

87. Veevers, J.E. (1972). **Factors in the Incidence of Childlessness in Canada: An Analysis of Census Data.** *Social Biology,* 19 (2).

88. Veevers, J.E. (1971). **Childlessness and Age at First Marriage.** *Social Biology,* 18 (3), pp. 292-295.

COHABITATION

89. Belliveau, J.A., Oderkirk, J. and Silver, C. (1994). **Common–law Unions: The Quebec Difference.** *Canadian Social Trends,* pp. 8-12.

90. Burch, T.K. (1989). **Common–law Unions in Canada: A Portrait from the 1984 Family History Survey.** In *The Family in Crisis: A Population Crisis?,* edited by J. Légaré, T.R. Balakrishnan and R.P. Beaujot, pp. 106-119. Ottawa: Lowe-Martin Company.

91. Fels, L. (1981). **Living Together: Unmarried Couples in Canada.** Toronto: Personal Library Publishers. "Non-marital cohabitation refers to an intimate relationship between two individuals of the opposite sex living together in a common residence outside of marriage."

92. Hall, D.R. and Zhao, J.Z. (1995). **Cohabitation and Divorce in Canada: Testing the Selectivity Hypothesis.** *Journal of Marriage and the Family,* 57, pp. 421-427.

93. Halli, S.S. and Zimmer, Z. (1991). **Common Law Unions as a Differentiating Factor in the Failure of Marriage in Canada, 1984.** *Social Indicators Research,* 24, pp. 329-345.

94. Hobart, C.W. (1983). **Marriage or Cohabitation.** In *Marriage and Divorce in Canada,* edited by K. Ishwaran, pp. 47-69. Toronto: Methuen.

95. Hobart, C.W. and Grigel, F. (1992). **Cohabitation Among Canadian Students at the End of the Eighties.** *Journal of Comparative Family Studies,* 23, pp. 311-337.

96. McKie, C. (1986). **Common–Law: Living Together as Husband and Wife.** *Canadian Social Trends,* pp. 39-41, Statistics Canada. A short discussion of the over 350,000 couples who lived together in 1981.

97. Stout, C. (1991). **Common–Law: A Growing Alternative.** *Canadian Social Trends,* 23, pp. 18-20.

98. Trussell, J. and Rao, K.V. (1989). **Premarital Cohabitation and Marital Stability: A Reassessment of the Canadian Evidence.** *Journal of Marriage and the Family,* 51, pp. 535-540.

99. Turcotte, P. (1988). **Common–Law Unions: Nearly Half a Million in 1986.** *Canadian Social Trends,* pp. 35-39.

100. Watson, R.E.L. (1983). **Premarital Cohabitation vs. Traditional Courtship: Their Effects on Subsequent Marital Adjustment.** *Family Relations,* 32, pp. 139-147.

101. White, J.M. (1987). **Premarital Cohabitation and Marital Stability in Canada.** *Journal of Marriage and the Family,* 49, pp. 641-648. The effect of premarital cohabitation on marriage is examined. Results suggest that cohabitation has a positive effect on staying married.

102. Wu, Z. (1999). **Premarital Cohabitation and the Timing of First Marriage.** *Canadian Review of Sociology and Anthropology,* 36 (1), pp. 109-128.

103. Wu, Z. and Balakrishnan, T.R. (1992). **Attitudes Towards Cohabitations and Marriage in Canada.** *Journal of Comparative Family Studies,* 23 (1), pp. 1-12.

COLLECTED READINGS ON FAMILY LIFE

104. Anderson, K.L. et al., eds. (1988). **Family Matters: Sociology and Contemporary Canadian Families.** Toronto: Nelson.

105. Anderson, K.L. et al. (1987). **Family Matters: Sociology and Contemporary Canadian Families.** Toronto: Methuen. Ten papers discuss varied aspects of family life in Canada. Historical aspects, parenting, social policy, divorce, violence, and the future of the family are some of the topics under discussion.

106. Baker, M., ed. (1990). **Families: Changing Trends in Canada, 2nd edition.** Toronto: McGraw-Hill Ryerson. Fourteen chapters review various aspects of Canadian family life.

107. Baker, M., ed. (1984). **The Family: Changing Trends in Canada.** Toronto: McGraw-Hill Ryerson. The eleven selections in this edited book of readings include the following topics: origins of the modern family, cultural variations in family structure, marriage dissolution, family violence, family and aging, family law, family and social policy, nontraditional family living, and the future of marriage.

108. Ishwaran, K., ed. (1983). **Marriage and Divorce in Canada.** Toronto: Methuen. Fourteen authors discuss selected aspects of Canadian marriage and divorce.

109. Ishwaran, K., ed. (1983). **The Canadian Family.** Toronto: Gage. A collection of 23 articles dealing with varied aspects of Canadian family life.

110. Ishwaran, K., ed. (1980). **Canadian Families: Ethnic Variations.** Toronto: McGraw-Hill Ryerson. Fourteen selections review specific ethnic groups in Canada.

111. Ishwaran, K., ed. (1979). **Childhood and Adolescence in Canada**. Toronto: McGraw-Hill Ryerson Limited. This book contains a compilation of various studies on childhood and adolescence from a socialization process point of view. A total of 15 different papers are presented. They include presentations from an interdisciplinary perspective (psychology, sociology, and anthropology).

112. Ishwaran, K., ed. (1971). **The Canadian Family.** Toronto: Holt, Rinehart and Winston. Twenty-nine contributors discuss various aspects of Canadian family life. This book of readings was a "first" in Canada.

113. Paterson, G.H., ed. (1988). **Children and Death.** London: King's College. Thirty-seven contributors discuss various aspects related to bereaved parents and surviving siblings.

114. Ramu, G., ed. (1988). **Marriage and the Family in Canada Today.** Toronto: Prentice-Hall Canada. A book of readings related to Canadian family life. The topics include courtship, marriage, work and family life, ethnicity, aging, divorce, family law, and alternative lifestyles.

115. Ramu, G.N., ed. (1993). **Marriage and the Family in Canada Today, 2nd edition.** Toronto: Prentice-Hall Canada. Twelve papers discuss various aspects of family life.

116. Ramu, G.N., ed. (1979). **Courtship, Marriage and the Family in Canada.** Toronto: Macmillan of Canada. Eleven selections discuss various aspects of the topic.

117. Tepperman, L. and Curtis, J., eds. (1988). **Readings in Sociology.** Toronto: McGraw-Hill Ryerson. Section 9 (pp. 415-478) contains six selections dealing with women and the family, marriage, and births.

118. Veevers, J.E., ed. (1991). **Continuity and Change in Marriage and Family.** Toronto: Holt, Rinehart and Winston.

119. Wakil, S.P., ed. (1975). **Marriage, Family and Society: Canadian Perspectives.** Toronto: Butterworths. This book of readings contains 29 selections that have a Canadian perspective.

DATA BASE RELATED TO FAMILIES

120. National Information Services Corporation (1999). *Family Studies Database (FSD).* Family Studies Database (FSD) is the premier electronic finding aid and index to family research, policy and practical literature. Annual subscriptions are available via the Internet (WWW) and CD-ROM. This database has more than 240,000 abstracts and citations. The Family Studies Database is the most

comprehensive index to family-related literature available, featuring the Inventory of Marriage & Family Literature (formerly published in print), Family Resources (formerly available online) and the well-respected Australian Family & Society Abstracts. National Information Services Corporation, 3100 St. Paul Street, Baltimore, Maryland, 21218, USA, Tel: (410) 243-0797, Fax: (410) 243-0982, email: sales@nisc.com.

DEMOGRAPHIC TRENDS

121. Adams, O. (1988). **Divorce Rates in Canada.** *Canadian Social Trends*, 11, pp. 18-21. A short analysis of the Canadian divorce trends in 1986.

122. Adams, O.B. and Nagnur, D.N. (1990). **Marrying and Divorce: A Status Report for Canada.** In *Canadian Social Trends,* edited by C. McKie and K. Thompson. Toronto: Thompson Educational Press.

123. Adams, O.B. and Nagnur, D.N. (1988). **Marriage, Divorce and Mortality: A Life Table Analysis.** Catalogue 84-536E. Ottawa: Statistics Canada, Minister of Supply and Services.

124. Barr, L. (1993). **Basic Facts of Families in Canada, Past and Present.** Catalogue 89-516. Ottawa: Statistics Canada, Housing, Family and Social Statistics Division.

125. Basavarajappa, K.G. (1978). **Marital Status and Nuptility in Canada.** Catalogue 99-704. Ottawa: Statistics Canada.

126. Beaujot, R. (1990). **The Family and Demographic Change in Canada: Economic and Cultural Interpretations and Solutions.** *Journal of Comparative Family Studies,* 21 (1), pp. 25-38.

127. Beaujot, R. (1988). **The Family in Crisis?** *The Canadian Journal of Sociology,* 13, pp. 305-311. A summary of a 1986 meeting of Canadian demographers.

128. Beaujot, R. (1986). **Dwindling Families.** *Policy Options,* 7, pp. 3-7.

129. Beaujot, R., Gee, E.M., Rajulton, F. and Ravanera, Z.R. (1995). **Family Life over the Life Course.** Ottawa: Statistics Canada. Selected family trends in Canadian society are discussed in this monograph, including family patterns in mid-life.

130. Beaujot, R.P. and McQuillan, K. (1986). **The Social Effects of Demographic Change: Canada 1851–1981.** *Journal of Canadian Studies,* 21, pp. 57-69.

131. Boyd, M. (1983). **The Social Demography of Divorce in Canada.** In *Marriage and Divorce in Canada,* edited by K. Ishwaran. Toronto: Methuen.

132. Boyd, M. (1974). **Family Size Ideals of Canadians: A Methodological Note.** *Canadian Review of Sociology and Anthropology,* 11 (4), pp. 360-370.

133. Burch, T.K. (1986). **Family History Survey: Preliminary Findings.** Ottawa: Ministry of Supply and Services.

134. Burch, T.K. (1985). **Family History Survey: Preliminary Findings.** Ottawa: Statistics Canada. Longitudinal data related to family patterns in Canada.

135. Caitlin, G., Mazikins, B., Moore, M. and Priest, G. (1989). **The 1984 Family History Survey: An Overview.** In *The Family in Crisis,* edited by J. Légaré, T.R. Balakrishnan, and R. Beajot, pp. 53-62. Ottawa: Royal Society of Canada.

136. Chalam-Zukewich, N. (1996). **Living with Relatives.** *Canadian Social Trends,* pp. 20-24. In 1991 in Canada, three percent of the total population lived with relatives. This is most common among seniors. Six percent of seniors aged 65-74 lived with relatives.

137. Charles, E. (1948). **The Changing Size of the Family in Canada.** Ottawa: Statistics Canada. A discussion of the 1941 census data.

138. Che-Alford, J., Allan, C. and Butlin, G. (1994). **Families in Canada.** An analysis of the 1991 census data related to families.

139. Devereaux, M.S. (1988). **1986 Census Highlights: Marital Status.** *Canadian Social Trends,* pp. 24-27. A statistical review related to marital status in Canada, from the 1986 census.

140. Devereaux, M.S. (1987). **Aging of the Canadian Population.** *Canadian Social Trends,* pp. 38-48. A short demographic analysis of Canada's aging population.

141. Dominion Bureau of Statistics (1967). **Life Expectancy Trends: 1930–32 to 1960–62.** Catalogue 84-518. Ottawa: Dominion Bureau of Statistics.

142. Dumas, J. (1994). **Report on the Demographic Situation in Canada 1993.** Ottawa: Statistics Canada (Cat. #91-209 E).

143. Dumas, J. (1987). **Report on the Demographic Situation in Canada 1986.** Ottawa: Ministry of Supply and Services. (Cat. #91-209 E). A monograph by Statistics Canada that examines demographic trends in Canada in 1986.

144. Dumas, J. (1984). **Report on the Demographic Situation in Canada 1983.** Ottawa: Ministry of Supply and Services. Major demographic trends are discussed

in this monograph including births, deaths, marriage and divorce, and life expectancy at birth.

145. Dumas, J. and Bélanger, A. (1994). **Report on the Demographic Situation in Canada 1994. The Sandwich Generation: Myths and Reality.** Ottawa: Statistics Canada (Cat. #91-209 E). A detailed analysis of the demographic Canadian trends related to the Sandwich Generation. (Marketing, Sales and Services, Statistics Canada, Ottawa, Ontario, K1A OT6).

146. Dumas, J. and Lavoie, Y. (1992). **Report on the Demographic Situation in Canada 1992.** Ottawa: Statistics Canada (Cat. #91-209 E).

147. Dumas, J. and Peron, Y. (1992). **Marriage and Conjugal Life in Canada.** Ottawa: Statistics Canada.

148. Health Reports (1992). **Divorce, 1990, Supplement No. 17.** Catalogue 82-003S16. Ottawa: Statistics Canada.

149. Health Reports (1992). **Marriages, 1990, Supplement No. 16.** Catalogue 82-003S16. Ottawa: Statistics Canada.

150. Kalbach, W. and McVey, W.W. (1979). **The Demographic Basis of Canadian Society, 2nd edition.** Toronto: McGraw-Hill Ryerson. (First edition 1971).

151. La Novara, P. (1993). **A Portrait of Families in Canada.** Ottawa: Statistics Canada, Catalogue 89-523E.

152. Lindsay, C. (1992). **Lone–Parent Families in Canada.** Catalogue 89-522E. Ottawa: Minister of Industry, Science and Technology.

153. Lindsay, C. and Belliveau, J.A. (1985). **Women in Canada: A Statistical Report.** Catalogue 89-503E. Ottawa: Statistics Canada, Social and Economic Studies Division.

154. McKie, C. and Thompson, K., ed. (1990). **Canadian Social Trends: Volume 1.** Toronto: Thompson Educational Publishing. Unit 2 discusses demographic trends related to Canadian families.

155. McMaster University (1996). **Focus on Aging in Canada.** Hamilton: Office of Gerontological Studies. A comprehensive demographic profile of the elderly (65+) population in Canada. A unique reference tool for studying this age cohort.

156. Moore, E.G., Rosenberg, M.W. and McGuinness, D. (1997). **Growing Old in Canada: Demographic and Geographic Perspectives.** Toronto: Nelson. This book explores older Canadians' lives today and tomorrow. It is a monograph produced by Statistics Canada as part of the 1991 Census Program.

157. Pelletier, A.J., Thomson, F.D. and Rochon, A. (1931). **The Canadian Family: A Study Based on the Census of 1931 and Supplementary Data.** Ottawa: J.O. Patenoude.

158. Ram, B. (1990). **New Trends in the Family. Demographic Facts and Figures.** Prepared for Statistics Canada, Catalogue 91-535E. Ottawa: Minister of Supply and Services Canada.

159. Ram, B. and Romaniuc, A. (1991). **Current Demographic Analysis: New Trends in the Family.** Ottawa: Minister of Supply and Services.

160. Rodgers, R.A. and Witney, G. (1981). **The Family Life Cycle in Twentieth Century Canada.** *Journal of Marriage and the Family,* 43, pp. 727-740. This articles focuses on a comparative study between Canadian and American families. They use data from Canadian Census and Vital Statistics.

161. Romanuic, A. (1984). **Current Demographic Analysis. Fertility in Canada: From Baby Boom to Baby Bust.** Ottawa: Minister of Supply and Services, Catalogue 91-524E.

162. Statistics Canada (1995). **Women in Canada: A Statistical Report.** Ottawa: Statistics Canada.

163. Statistics Canada (1994). **Characteristics of Dual–Earner Families, 1992.** Catalogue 13-213. Ottawa: Ministry of Industry, Science and Technology.

164. Statistics Canada (1994). **Women in the Labour Force.** Catalogue 75-507. Ottawa: Statistics Canada.

165. Statistics Canada (1990). **Women in Canada: A Statistical Report, 2nd edition.** Ottawa: Statistics Canada.

166. Statistics Canada (1987). **Census Canada 1986: Summary, Tabulations: Canada, Provinces, and Territories.** Ottawa: Statistics Canada. The data was collected from all households. A complete set of data related to families living in Canadian households.

167. Statistics Canada (1985). **Women in Canada: A Statistical Report.** Ottawa: Ministry of Supply and Services. This report statistically describes the major aspects of women's lives including their family status, education, and health and work experience since 1970.

168. Statistics Canada (1984). **Canada's Lone–Parent Families.** Ottawa. This is a family studies teaching kit that includes complete statistics of the 1981 census, charts, and transparencies. (Cat. #11-520 E).

169. Statistics Canada (1984). **Canada's Young Family Homeowners**. Ottawa. A family studies teaching kit that includes census data from 1981. It also has transparencies for the teacher. (Cat. #11-517 E).

170. Statistics Canada (1984). **Living Alone.** Ottawa. A family studies teaching kit that includes data and charts related to the 1981 census. Transparencies are also included for the teacher. (Cat. #11-515 E).

171. Statistics Canada (1984). **The Elderly in Canada.** Ottawa: Minister of Supply and Services. This is a family studies teaching kit that contains the 1981 census data. Transparencies are also included. (Cat. #11-519 E).

172. Statistics Canada (1983). **Fact Book on Aging in Canada.** Ottawa: Minister of Supply and Services.

173. Statistics Canada (1979). **Canada's Families.** Ottawa: Minister of Supply and Services.

174. Statistics Canada (1978). **Families by Family Structure and Family Type.** Ottawa. Catalogue 93-822. A summary of the 1976 Census data.

175. Statistics Canada (1973). **1971 Census: Women Ever Married by Number of Children.** Catalogue 92-718.

176. Statistics Canada (1963). **1961 Census: Husband–Wife Families.** Catalogue 93-250.

177. Thompson Educational Publishing (1994). **Canadian Social Trends: Volume 2.** Toronto: Thompson Educational Publishing. Units 5 and 6 discuss demographic trends related to Canadian marriages and families.

DIVORCE: CUSTODY

178. Ambert, A.M. (1985). **Custodial Parents: Review and a Longitudinal Study.** In *The One Parent Family in the 1980s,* edited by B. Schlesinger. Toronto: University of Toronto Press.

179. Ambert, A.M. (1982). **Differences in Children's Behavior Toward Custodial Mothers and Fathers.** *Journal of Marriage and the Family*, 44, pp. 73-86.

180. Ambert, A.M. (1982). **Differences in Children's Behaviour Towards Custodial Mothers and Custodial Fathers.** *Journal of Marriage and the Family*, 44, pp. 73-86. This study looked at the interaction between children's behaviour and socio-

demographic characteristics (sex and socio-economic status) of custodial parents in situations involving divorce or separation.

181. Benjamin, M. and Irving, H. (1984). **Shared Parenting: A Critical Review of the Research.** *Canadian Social Work Review,* 1, pp. 13-29. A review of the literature on shared parenting.

182. Bourque, D.M. (1995). **"Reconstructing" the Patriarchal Nuclear Family: Recent Developments in Child Custody and Access in Canada.** *Canadian Journal of Law and Society,* 10, pp. 1-24.

183. Dennis, W. (1998). **The Divorce From Hell: How the Justice System Failed a Family.** Toronto: Macfarlane Walter & Ross.

184. Drakich, J. (1988). **In Whose Best Interest? The Politics of Joint Custody.** In *Family Bonds and Gender Divisions,* edited by B. Fox. Toronto: Canadian Scholars' Press.

185. Fineman, M.L. (1989). **Custody Determination at Divorce: The Limits of Social Science Research and the Fallacy of the Liberal Ideology of Equality.** *Canadian Journal of Women and the Law,* 3 (1), pp. 134-154.

186. Green, D. (1982). **Joint Custody and the Emerging Two–Parent Family.** *Conciliation Courts Review,* 21, pp. 65-75. A plea that children should be involved with both parents after the divorce.

187. Irving, H. and Benjamin, M. (1986). **Shared Parenting in Canada: Questions, Answers and Implications.** *Canadian Family Law Quarterly,* 1, pp. 79-100. A report of a study of 201 shared parents and 194 sole custody parents.

188. Irving, H., Benjamin, M. and Trocme, N. (1984). **Shared Parenting: An Empirical Analysis Utilizing a Large Data Base.** *Family Process,* 23, pp. 561-569. The results of a study of 201 Canadian parents involved in shared parenting arrangements.

189. Pearson, L. and Gallaway, R. (1998). **For the Sake of Children.** Ottawa: Senate of Canada. The Report of the Special Joint Committee on Child Custody and Access.

190. Schlesinger, B. (1977). **Children and Divorce in Canada.** *Journal of Divorce,* 2, pp. 175-182.

DIVORCE: MEDIATION

191. Department of Justice, Canada (1988). **Another Way: Mediation in Divorce and Separation.** Ottawa: Department of Justice, Canada. A booklet describing mediation services in Canada.

192. Devlin, A. and Ryan, J.P. (1986). **Family Mediation in Canada: Past, Present and Future Development.** *International Developments in Divorce Mediation Quarterly,* 11, pp. 93-108.

193. Irving, H. (1980). **Divorce Mediation: The Rational Alternative.** Toronto: Personal Library. A discussion of divorce mediation.

194. Irving, H. and Benjamin, M. (1987). **Family Mediation: Theory and Practice of Dispute Resolution.** Toronto: Carswell. A resource book dealing with family mediation.

195. Landau, B. (1988). **Mediation: An Option for Divorcing Families.** *Advocate's Quarterly,* 9, pp. 1-21.

196. Richardson, C.J. (1987). **Divorce and Family Mediation Research Study in Three Canadian Cities.** Ottawa: Department of Justice.

DIVORCE: OVERVIEW

197. Ambert, A.M. (1999). **Divorce: Facts, Figures and Consequences.** Ottawa: Vanier Institute of the Family. *Contemporary Family Trends* (a position paper). An examination of divorce in Canada, including existing demographic trends and research findings.

198. Ambert, A.M. (1990). **Marriage Dissolution: Structural and Ideological Changes.** In *Families: Changing Trends in Canada,* 2nd edition, edited by M. Baker. Toronto: McGraw-Hill Ryerson.

199. Ambert, A.M. (1989). **Ex–Spouses and New Spouses: A Study of Relationships.** Greenwich: JAI Press.

200. Ambert, A.M. (1988). **Relationship Between Ex–Spouses: Individual and Dyadic Perspectives.** *Journal of Social and Personal Relationships,* 5, pp. 327-346.

201. Ambert, A.M. (1988). **Relationship with Former In–laws after Divorce: A Research Note.** *Journal of Marriage and the Family,* 50, pp. 679-686. A study of how divorce affects the relationships with former relatives by marriage.

202. Ambert, A.M. (1985). **The Effect of Divorce on Women's Attitude Toward Feminism.** *Sociological Focus,* 18, pp. 265-272.

203. Ambert, A.M. (1980). **Divorce in Canada.** Toronto: Longman. A complete discussion of divorce in Canada, including a review of the literature.

204. Baker, M. (1984). **His and Her Divorce Research: New Theoretical Directions in Canadian and American Research.** *Journal of Comparative Family Studies,* 15, pp. 17-28. A plea to include women's studies as part of Canadian family research. In Canada most family articles were written by men who use a more conservative theoretical framework.

205. Baker, M. (1983). **Divorce: Its Consequences and Meanings.** In *The Canadian Family,* edited by K. Ishwaran, pp. 289-300. Toronto: Gage.

206. Finnie, R. (1993). **Women, Men and the Economic Consequences of Divorce: Evidence from Canadian Longitudinal Data.** *Canadian Review of Sociology and Anthropology,* 30 (2), pp. 205-241.

207. Frosst, S. and Thomson, W. (1980). **A Study of Concerns of Divorcing Women.** *Canadian Journal of Social Work Education,* 6 (2-3), pp. 25-44. A study of 128 francophone women in Quebec who used the Legal Aid Service.

208. Huddleston, R.J. and Hawkins, L. (1986). **The Effect of Divorce: A Study of the Reports of Divorced Albertans.** *Conciliation Courts Review,* 24 pp. 59-68. A study of 21 persons (7 males, 14 females) to examine the effects of divorce on their lives.

209. Lero, D.S. (1981). **A Different Understanding: Divorce a Family Crisis.** Toronto: TV Ontario. An overview of current research on the subject of children of divorce.

210. Malcabe, T. (1980). **Provincial Variations in Divorce Rates: A Canadian Case.** *Journal of Marriage and the Family,* 42, pp. 171-176. It has become clear that since the enactment of new divorce legislation in 1968 that divorce rates vary between the provinces in Canada.

211. Peters, J. (1987). **Changing Perspectives on Divorce.** In *Family Matters,* edited by K.J. Anderson et al. Toronto: Methuen, pp. 141-162. A discussion of divorce in Canada prior to the changes in 1968, and the present 1986 situation.

212. Peters, J. (1980). **Divorce.** In *Courtship, Marriage and the Family in Canada,* edited by G.N. Ramu, pp. 134-152. Toronto: Gage.

213. Peters, J.F. (1979). **Divorce.** Toronto: Guidance Centre, Faculty of Education, University of Toronto. This booklet discusses divorce in Canada.

214. Peters, J.F. (1976). **Divorce in Canada: A Demographic Profile.** *Journal of Comparative Family Studies,* 7 (2), pp. 335-349.

215. Pike, R. (1975). **Legal Access and the Incidence of Divorce in Canada: A Sociohistorical Analysis.** *Canadian Review of Sociology and Anthropology,* 12, pp. 115-133.

216. Proulx, J. and Koulack, D. (1987). **The Effect of Parental Divorce on Parent–Adolescent Separation.** *Journal of Youth and Adolescence,* 16, pp. 473-480.

217. Richardson, C.J. (1988). **Children of Divorce.** In *Family Matters,* edited by K.L. Anderson et al. Toronto: Nelson.

218. Robson, B. (1979). **My Parents are Divorced Too.** Toronto: Dorset Publishing. A psychiatrist interviews 28 young people who underwent separation and divorce.

219. Sevér, A. (1992). **Women and Divorce in Canada, A Sociological Analysis.** Toronto: Canadian Scholars' Press.

220. Trovato, F. (1986). **The Relationship between Migration and the Provincial Divorce Rate in Canada, 1971 and 1978: A Reassessment.** *Journal of Marriage and the Family,* 48, pp. 207-216. Regions that are characterized by high rates of population mobility have high divorce rates.

221. Troyer, W. (1979). **Divorced Kids.** Toronto: Clarke, Irwin. A divorced father interviews children of divorce. The children reply with candor and with humour about their adjustment to divorce.

ECONOMICS AND FAMILY LIFE

222. Armstrong, P. (1990). **Economic Conditions and Family Structures.** In *Families: Changing Trends in Canada,* 2nd edition, edited by M. Baker. Toronto: McGraw-Hill Ryerson.

223. Bradbury, B. (1992). **Gender at Work at Home: Family Decisions, the Labour Market and Girls' Contributions to the Family Economy.** In *Canadian Family History,* edited by B. Bradbury. Toronto: Copp-Clark Pitman.

224. Bridge, K. (1986). **An International Survey of Private and Public Law Maintenance of Single–Parent Families: Summary and Recommendations.**

Ottawa: Ministry of Supply and Services. This study reviews the economic situation of the single-parent family in Canada.

225. Cheal, D.J. (1983). **Intergenerational Family Transfers.** *Journal of Marriage and the Family,* 45, pp. 805-813.

226. Cowan, B. (1987). **Manual on Curriculum Planning and Development: Economics in the Family.** Toronto: Ontario Family Studies Educators Association. A sample guide to planning curriculum developments.

227. Dulude, L. (1984). **Love, Marriage and Money... An Analysis of Financial Arrangements between the Spouses.** Ottawa: Canadian Advisory Council on the Status of Women.

228. Kingsmill, S. and Stuart, S. (1998). **Breaking Up Solvent: A Woman's Guide to Financial Security.** Calgary: Delselig Enterprises. A discussion about divorce in Canada and the financial aspects of the divorce process.

229. McCall, M.L., Hornick, J.P. and Wallace, J.E. (1988). **The Process and Economic Consequences of Marriage Breakdown.** Calgary: Canadian Research Institute for Law and the Family.

230. Mitchell, A. (1987). **The Cost of Raising a Child in the Toronto Area in 1986.** *Social Infopac,* 6 (5), pp. 1-5. Social Planning Council of Metropolitan Toronto.

231. Morrison, R.J. and Oderkirk, J. (1991). **Married and Unmarried Couples: The Tax Question.** *Canadian Social Trends,* pp. 15-20.

232. Pask, E.D. and McCall, M.L. (1989). **How Much and Why? Economic Implications of Marriage Breakdown: Spousal and Child Support.** Calgary: Canadian Research Institute for Law and Family.

233. Sauvé, R. (1999). **Trends in Canadian Family Incomes, Expenditures, Savings and Debt.** Ottawa: Vanier Institute of the Family. *Contemporary Family Trends* (a position paper). A broader and longer-term picture of how families have fared financially during the past 50 years.

234. Tremblay, M. and Fortin, G. (1964). **Economic Behaviour of the Middle Class Family of Quebec.** Quebec: University of Laval Press.

235. Wilson, J.J. (1986). **Women, The Family and the Economy**, 2nd edition. Toronto: McGraw-Hill Ryerson. An examination of a feminist view of women and the family in Canada.

ETHNIC FAMILY LIFE

236. Abu-Laban, S. (1980). **Arab–Canadian Family Life.** In *An Olive Branch on the Family Tree,* edited by B. Abu-Laban, pp. 158-180. Toronto: McClelland and Stewart.

237. Ames, M.M. and Inglis, J. (1976). **Tradition and Change in British Columbia Sikh Family Life.** In *The Canadian Family Revisited,* edited by K. Ishwaran. Toronto: Holt, Rinehart and Winston, 1976, pp. 77-91. Changes in traditional Sikh family structure resulting from adjustment to settlement in British Columbia are examined from the perspective of the stresses and conflicts underlying those changes.

238. Anderson, A. and Driedger, L. (1980). **The Mennonite Family: Culture and Kin in Rural Saskatchewan.** In *Canadian Families: Ethnic Variations,* edited by K. Ishwaran. Toronto: McGraw-Hill Ryerson.

239. Ashworth, M. (1993). **Children of the Canadian Mosaic.** Toronto: OISE Press.

240. Barclay, H.B. (1976). **The Lebanese Muslim Family.** In *The Canadian Family Revisited,* edited by K. Ishwaran. Toronto: Holt, Rinehart and Winston, 1976, pp. 92-104. A brief review of the Muslim conception of family and marriage present the family as a male-centered and patriarchal system.

241. Bhargava, G. (1988). **Seeking Immigration Through Matrimonial Alliance: A Study of Advertisements in an Ethnic Weekly.** *Journal of Comparative Family Studies,* 19, pp. 245-249.

242. Boissevain, J. (1976). **Family and Kinship Among Italians in Montreal.** In *The Canadian Family,* revised edition, edited by K. Ishwaran. Toronto: Holt, Rinehart and Winston.

243. Boissevain, J. (1975). **Family, Kinship and Marriage Among Italians of Montreal.** In *Marriage, Family and Society,* edited by S.P. Wakil, pp. 287-294. Toronto: Butterworths.

244. Boissevain, J. (1970). **The Italians of Montreal. Social Adjustment in a Plural Society.** Ottawa: Queen's Printer.

245. Bond, J.B., Harvey, C.D.H. and Hildebrand, E. (1987). **Familial Support of the Elderly in a Rural Mennonite Community.** *Canadian Journal of Aging,* 6, pp. 7-18. A study of support from middle-age offspring to elderly persons in a rural Mennonite community.

246. Briggs, J.L. (1970). **Never in Anger: Portrait of an Eskimo Family.** Cambridge, MA: Harvard University Press.

247. Canadian Historical Association (1982-85). **Canada's Ethnic Groups.** Ottawa: Canadian Historical Association. The following booklets are available:

    - J. Tan and P.E. Roy. **The Chinese in Canada.** 1985.
    - H. Johnston. **The East Indians in Canada.** 1984.
    - V. Lindstrom-Best. **The Finns in Canada.** 1985.
    - K.M. McLaughlin. **The Germans in Canada.** 1985.
    - D. Higgs. **The Portuguese in Canada.** 1982.
    - W.P. Ward. **The Japanese in Canada.** 1982.
    - B.L. Vigod. **The Jews in Canada.** 1984.
    - J.M. Bumsted. **The Scots in Canada.** 1982.
    - D.H. Avery and J.K. Federowicz. **The Poles in Canada.** 1982.
    - O.W. Gerus and J.E. Really. **The Ukrainians in Canada.** 1985.
    - J.W. St. G. Walker. **The West Indians in Canada.** 1984.

    The price per booklet is $2.00. Each contains a selected bibliography.

248. Chimbos, P.D. (1980). **The Greek–Canadian Family.** In *Canadian Families: Ethnic Variations,* edited by K. Ishwaran. Toronto: McGraw-Hill Ryerson Limited, pp. 27-41. This paper examines some aspects of family life among Greek Canadians.

249. Christensen, C. and Weinfeld, M. (1993). **The Black Family in Canada: A Preliminary Exploration of Family Patterns and Inequality.** *Canadian Ethnic Studies,* 24 (3), pp. 26-44.

250. Christiansen, J.M., Thornley-Brown, A. and Robinson, J. (1981). **West Indians in Toronto.** Toronto: Family Service Association of Metropolitan Toronto. The number of West Indians living in Toronto has increased in recent years. The historical, social, and cultural background of this group is discussed in this book along with the migration process and methods of intervention for this group.

251. Cruikshank, J. (1971). **Matrifocal Families in the Canadian North.** In *The Canadian Family,* edited by K. Ishwaran, pp. 39-53. Toronto: Holt, Rinehart and Winston.

252. Damas, D. (1971). **The Problem of the Eskimo Family.** In *The Canadian Family,* edited by K. Ishwaran. Toronto: Holt, Rinehart and Winston.

253. Danziger, K. (1976). **The Acculturation of Immigrant Italian Girls.** In *The Canadian Family,* revised edited by K. Ishwaran. Toronto: Holt, Rinehart and Winston.

254. Danziger, K. (1971). **The Socialization of Immigrant Children.** Toronto: Institute of Behavioural Research, York University.

255. Disman, M. (1988). **Ethnicity and Aging.** Toronto: Programme in Gerontology, University of Toronto, 1988, Research Paper No. 9. A comprehensive review of the research literature on aging and ethnicity with an emphasis on Canadian studies.

256. Draper, P.J. and Karlinsky, J.B. (1986). **Abraham's Daughters: Women, Charity and Power in the Canadian Jewish Community.** In *Looking into My Sister's Eyes: An Exploration in Women's History,* edited by J. Burnet. Toronto: The Multicultural History Society of Ontario.

257. Driedger, L. and Chappell, N. (1987). **Aging and Ethnicity: Toward an Interface.** Toronto: Butterworths. This monograph looks at Canada's aging population with ethnic roots. Many ethnic families find themselves in the Sandwich Generation.

258. Dunning, R.W. (1971). **Changes in Marriage and the Family among the Northern Ojibwa.** In *The Canadian Family,* edited by K. Ishwaran. Toronto: Holt, Rinehart and Winston.

259. Elkin, F. (1985). **The English–Canadian Family.** In *The Family in Various Cultures*, 5th edition, edited by S. Queen, R.H. Habenstein and J.S. Quadgaguo. New York: Harper and Row, pp. 335-345. A discussion of family life in English-speaking Canada.

260. Elkin, F. (1983). **Family, Socialization, and Ethnic Identity.** In *The Canadian Family,* edited by K. Ishwaran, pp. 145-158. Toronto: Gage.

261. Gavaki, E. (1979). **The Greek Family in Canada: Continuity and Change and the Process of Adjustment.** *International Journal of Sociology of the Family,* 9 (1), pp. 1-16.

262. Gfellner, B.M. (1990). **Culture and Consistency in Ideal and Actual Child–Rearing Practices: A Study of Canadian Indian and White Parents.** *Journal of Comparative Family Studies,* 21, pp. 413-423.

263. Guemple, L. (1980). **Growing Old in Inuit Society.** In *Aging in Canada: Social Perspectives,* edited by Victor W. Marshall. Toronto: Fitzhenry and Whiteside Limited, pp. 95-102. This paper examines aging in Inuit society by describing the function of the family, roles of members with the family as well as the community, and how these roles change for the aged

264. Harney, N.D. (1998). **Eh Paesan! Being Italian in Toronto.** Toronto: University of Toronto Press.

265. Heinrich, A. (1972). **Divorce as an Integrative Social Factor Among Eskimos.** *Journal of Comparative Family Studies,* 3 (2), pp. 265-272.

266. Henry, F. (1994). **The Caribbean Diaspora in Toronto.** Toronto: University of Toronto Press.

267. Herbert, E.N. (1989). **Ethnic Groups in Canada: Adaptations and Transitions.** Toronto: Nelson Canada. Contains content related to ethnic family aspects.

268. Hobart, C.W. (1976). **The Changing Family Patterns among Ukrainian–Canadians in Alberta.** In *The Canadian Family in Comparative Perspective,* edited by L.E. Larson, pp. 351-365. Toronto: Prentice-Hall Canada.

269. Hobart, C.W. (1966). **Italian Immigrants in Edmonton: Adjustment and Integration.** Ottawa: Information Canada.

270. Ishwaran, K. (1977). **Family Kinship and Community: A Study of Dutch Canadians.** Toronto: McGraw-Hill Ryerson.

271. Ishwaran, K. (1976). **Family and Community Among the Dutch Canadians.** In *The Canadian Family,* revised edition, edited by K. Ishwaran, pp. 356-379. Toronto: Holt, Rinehart and Winston.

272. Jansen, C.J. (1971). **The Italian Community in Toronto.** In *Immigrant Groups,* Volume 2, edited by John L. Elliot. Scarborough: Prentice-Hall Canada.

273. Kallen, E. (1976). **Family Life Styles and Jewish Culture.** In *The Canadian Family,* revised edition, edited by K. Ishwaran. Toronto: Holt, Rinehart and Winston.

274. Kurokawa, M. (1971). **Mennonite Children in Waterloo County.** In *Immigrant Groups,* Volume 2, edited by John L. Elliot. Scarborough: Prentice-Hall Canada.

275. Kurokawa, M. (1969). **Psycho–Social Roles of Mennonite Children in a Changing Society.** *Canadian Review of Sociology and Anthropology,* 6 (1), pp. 15-35.

276. Lam, L. (1982). **The Chinese–Canadian Families of Toronto in 1970s.** *International Journal of Sociology of the Family,* 12 (1), pp. 11-32.

277. Latowsky (Kallen), E. (1971). **The Family Life Styles and Jewish Culture.** In *The Canadian Family,* edited by K. Ishwaran. Toronto: Holt, Rinehart and Winston.

278. Lewis, C. (1952). **Doukhobor Children and Family Life.** In *The Doukhobors of British Columbia,* edited by H.B. Hawthorn. Vancouver: University of British Columbia, pp. 97-121.

279. Li, P.S. (1988). **The Chinese in Canada.** Toronto: Oxford University Press.

280. Li, P.S. (1980). **Immigration Laws and Family Patterns: Some Demographic Changes Among Chinese in Canada.** *Canadian Ethnic Studies,* 11, pp. 70-77.

281. Matthiasson, J.S. (1980). **The Inuit Family: Past, Present and Future.** In *Canadian Families: Ethnic Variations,* edited by K. Ishwaran. Toronto: McGraw-Hill Ryerson.

282. Maykovich, M.K. (1976). **The Japanese Family in Tradition and Change.** In *The Canadian Family,* revised edition, edited by K. Ishwaran. Toronto: Holt, Rinehart and Winston.

283. McIrvin, Abu-Laban S. (1980). **Arab–Canadian Family Life.** In *An Olive Branch in the Family Tree,* edited by Baha Abu-Laban, pp. 158-180. Toronto: McClelland and Stewart.

284. Nagata, J. (1969). **Adaptation and Integration of Greek Working Class Immigrants in the City of Toronto: A Situational Analysis Approach.** *International Migration Review,* 4 (1), pp. 44-68.

285. Naidoo, J.C. and Davis, J.C. (1988). **Canadian South Asian Women in Transition: A Dualistic View of Life.** *Journal of Comparative Family Studies,* 19, pp. 311-328. The South Asian women are "traditional" with regard to family, religion, and marriage, but contemporary on values pertaining to education and development outside the home.

286. Ng, R. and Ramirez, J. (1981). **Immigrant Housewives in Canada.** Toronto: Immigrant Women's Centre.

287. Noivo, E. (1998). **Inside Ethnic Families: Three Generations of Portuguese–Canadians.** Montreal: McGill-Queen's University Press.

288. Peter, K. (1987). **The Dynamics of Hutterite Society: An Analytical Approach.** Edmonton: University of Alberta Press.

289. Peter, K. (1976). **The Hutterite Family.** In *The Canadian Family,* edited by K. Ishwaran. Toronto: Holt, Rinehart and Winston Limited, pp. 289-311. The approximately 20,000 Hutterites living in communal groups in North America are the descendants of only 18 families who in 1760 escaped religious persecution by migrating from Hungary to Russia. Two of the original family names have since died out. Kinship is patrilineal and patrilocal.

290. Peters, J. (1984). **Cultural Variations in Family Structure.** In *The Family: Changing Trends in Canada,* edited by M. Baker, pp. 63-84. Toronto: McGraw-Hill Ryerson. A brief analysis of selected ethnic families in Canada.

291. Price, J.A. (1985). **Canadian Ethnic Families.** In *The Canadian Family,* edited by K. Ishwaran. Toronto: Holt, Rinehart and Winston.

292. Radecki, H. (1980). **The Polish Canadian Family.** In *Canadian Families: Ethnic Variations,* edited by K. Ishwaran. Toronto: McGraw-Hill Ryerson, pp. 41-64. The aim of this article is to consider various dimensions of the Polish family in Canada. The scope of the inquiry includes phases and patters of immigration, background of family customs, traditions, and values in Poland, adjustment, and changes in the Polish family in Canada.

293. Radecki, H. (1976). **Polish Groups in Canada.** Toronto: McClelland and Stewart.

294. Radecki, H. (1970). **Polish–Canadian, Canadian–Polish, or Canadian?** Toronto: York University, Mimeograph.

295. Rashid, A. (1985). **The Muslim Canadians: A Profile.** Ottawa: Minister of Supply and Services.

296. Richard, M.A. (1991). **Ethnic Groups and Marital Choices**. Vancouver: University of British Columbia Press.

297. Richmond, A.H. (1967). **Immigrant and Ethnic Groups in Metropolitan Toronto.** Toronto: Institute for Behavioral Research, York University.

298. Rosenthal, C. (1986). **Intergenerational Solidarity in Later Life: Ethnic Contrasts in Jewish and Anglo Families.** Toronto: University of Toronto, Programme in Gerontology, Research Paper 4.

299. Rosenthal, C.J. (1987). **Family Supports in Later Life: Does Ethnicity Make a Difference?** *The Gerontologist,* 26, pp. 19-24. We have a lack of studies on ethnicity and family supports in later life. Various ethnic groups may have different approaches to elder care.

300. Schlesinger, B. and Forman, J. (1988). **Jewish Families: A Selected Review.** *Journal of Psychology and Judaism,* 12, pp. 90-109. A review of the literature dealing with Jewish family life in Canada and the United States.

301. Schoenfeld, S. (1988). **Integration into the Group and Sacred Uniqueness: Analysis of an Adult Bat Mitzvah.** In *Persistence and Flexibility,* edited by W.P. Zenner, Albany: State University of New York Press, pp. 117-136. A case history

of an adult woman who decided to have a Bat Mitzvah (Jewish ritual of coming of age).

302. Schoenfeld, S. (1983). **The Transmission of Jewish Identity Among Families in a Non–Jewish Neighborhood.** *Contemporary Jewry,* 6 (2), pp. 35-44. This article describes the Jewish identity of the families who have moved to downtown Toronto in the 1970s.

303. Siddique, C.M. (1977). **Changing Family Patterns: A Comparative Analysis of Immigrant Indian and Pakistani Families of Saskatoon, Canada.** *Journal of Comparative Family Studies,* 8, pp. 179-199.

304. Sturino, F. (1980). **Family and Kin Cohesion Among Southern Italian Immigrants.** In *Canadian Families: Ethnic Variations,* edited by K. Ishwaran. Toronto: McGraw-Hill Ryerson.

305. Sturino, F. (1980). **The Southern Italian Immigrants in Toronto.** In *Canadian Families: Ethnic Variations,* edited by K. Ishwaran. Toronto: McGraw-Hill Ryerson, pp. 84-104. It is the purpose of this paper to explore some of the ways that Italians who immigrated to Toronto after World War II, through kinship chains, have been able to preserve family and kindred cohesiveness in the face of a New World environment while at the same time adjusting to it.

306. Tastsoglou, E. and Stubos, G. (1993). **The Greek Immigrant Family in the United States and Canada: The Transition from an "Institutional" to a "Relational" Form (1945–1970).** *Journal of International Migration,* 30 (2), pp. 155-173.

307. Thomas, G. (1988). **Women in the Greek Community of Nova Scotia.** *Canadian Ethnic Studies,* 20 (3), pp. 84-93.

308. Verma, R., Chan, K.G. and Lam, L. (1980). **The Chinese–Canadian Family: A Socio–Economic Profile.** In *Canadian Families: Ethnic Variations,* edited by K. Ishwaran. Toronto: McGraw-Hill Ryerson Limited, pp. 138-157. This paper examines the social, economic, and demographic characteristics of Chinese immigrants in Canada by using the census data and 1966–75 immigration statistics.

309. Wakil, S.P., Siddique, C. and Wakil, F.A. (1981). **Between Two Cultures: A Study in Socialization of Children of Immigrants.** *Journal of Marriage and the Family,* 42, pp. 829-940.

310. Woon, Y.F. (1986). **Some Adjustment Aspects of Vietnamese and Sino–Vietnamese Families in Victoria, Canada.** *Journal of Comparative Family Studies,* 17, pp. 349-370. A study of 50 families from Vietnam examines their adjustment to Canadian society.

311. Young, M.M. and Ishwaran, K. (1978). **Family, Kinship and Community: A Study of Dutch–Canadians.** *American Anthropologist,* 80 (3), p. 695.

FAMILY CAREGIVING

312. Aronson, J. (1991). **Dutiful Daughters and Undemanding Mothers: Constraining Images of Giving and Receiving Care in Middle and Later Life.** In *Women's Caring: Feminist Perspectives on Social Welfare,* edited by C.T. Baines, P.M. Evans and S.M. Neysmith, pp. 138-168. Toronto: McClelland and Stewart. In Canada, 85 to 90 percent of the care of elderly persons is provided informally by their families. Mostly women are the care providers. Case studies illustrate the work of the "caretaker."

313. Aronson, J. (1985). **Family Care of the Elderly: Underlying Assumptions and Their Consequences.** *Canadian Journal of Aging,* 4, pp. 115-125.

314. Carnet (1993). **Work and Family: The Survey.** The Canadian Aging Research Network. A Canadian study of 5,121 respondents from eight organizations. The findings were related to elder care of employees in these organization. Forty-six percent were involved in elder care.

315. Chappell, N.L. and Litkenhaus, R. (1995). **Informal Caregivers to Adults in British Columbia.** Joint report of the Centre on Aging, University of Victoria, and the Caregivers Association of British Columbia. A study of informal caregivers in British Columbia.

316. Frederick, J.A. and Fast, J.E. (1999). **Eldercare in Canada: Who Does How Much?** *Canadian Social Trends,* 54, Autumn, 26-30. A study of 1,366 caregiver/care receiver dyads. Women do the bulk of eldercare.

317. Globerman, J. (1996). **The Case of Daughters–in–Law and Sons–in–Law in the Care of Relatives with Alzheimer's Disease.** *Family Relations,* 45 (1), pp. 37-45.

318. Globerman, J. (1994). **Balancing Tensions in Families with Alzheimer's Disease: The Self and the Family.** *Journal of Aging Studies,* 8, pp. 211-232.

319. Keating, N., Kerr, K., Warren, S., Grace, M. and Wertenberger, D. (1994). **Who's the Family in Family Caregiving?** *Canadian Journal on Aging,* 13 (2), pp. 268-287.

320. Keefe, J.M. and Blain, J.M.M. (1995). **Partnerships in Care: The Involvement of Family Members with Elderly Relatives in Homes for Special Care.** Halifax:

Nova Scotia Centre on Aging, Mount Saint Vincent University. A study of 214 Nova Scotia families who had an elderly family member in an institution.

321. Statistics Canada (1997). **Who Cares? Caregiving in the 1990s.** *The Daily,* 29, pp. 4-5. A report on women and men who are caregivers in Canada. Of all the women who lived with a spouse and children, 16 percent were caregivers to elderly parents. The largest percentage of caregivers were women in the 45–64 age group.

322. Walker, A.J. (1991). **The Relationship between the Family and the State in the Care of Older People.** *Canadian Journal on Aging,* 10 (2), pp. 94-113.

FAMILY LIFE: OVERVIEW

323. Conway, J.F. (1990). **The Canadian Family in Crisis.** Toronto: James Lorimer & Co.

324. Crysdale, S. (1976). **Workers' Families and Education in a Downtown Community.** In *The Canadian Family,* revised edition, edited by K. Ishwaran. Toronto: Holt, Rinehart and Winston.

325. Crysdale, S. (1968). **Family and Kinship in Riverdale.** In *Canada,* edited by W.E. Mann. Toronto: Copp Clark.

326. Davids, L. (1980). **Family Change in Canada: 1971–1976.** *Journal of Marriage and the Family,* 42 (1), pp. 177-183.

327. Eichler, M. (1988). **Families in Canada Today: Recent Changes and Their Policy Consequences, 2nd edition.** Toronto: Gage.

328. Eichler, M. and Bullen, M. (1986). **Families in Canada: An Introduction.** Toronto: OISE Press. Examines the myths and realities of Canadian families in the past and in the present.

329. Elkin, F. (1964). **The Family in Canada.** Ottawa: Vanier Institute of the Family. The classic book that began Canada's concern with research on families.

330. Erwin, A.J. (1967). **Families.** Toronto: General Publishing Co. Ltd.

331. Eshleman, J.R. and Wilson, S.J. (1994). **The Family: Canadian Edition.** Toronto: Allyn and Bacon. An introductory family textbook. Originally published in the United States and adapted to Canadian society.

332. Gaffield, C. (1990). **The Social and Economic Origins of Contemporary Families.** In *Families: Changing Trends in Canada,* 2nd edition, edited by M. Baker. Toronto: McGraw-Hill Ryerson.

333. Gairdner, W. (1992). **The War Against the Family: A Parent Speaks Out.** Toronto: Stoddart.

334. Hanson, K. and Gower, E. (1988). **People in Society.** Toronto: Holt, Rinehart and Winston of Canada. This book for secondary school students includes a section on the Canadian family (177-208).

335. Jones, C.L., Tepperman, L. and Wilson, S.J. (1995). **The Futures of the Family.** Toronto: Prentice-Hall Canada. An analysis of some historical aspects of the family, including marriage, childbearing, parenting, and changing family forms. Contains little content about Canada.

336. Kalbach, W.E. (1983). **The Canadian Family: A Profile.** In *The Canadian Family,* edited by K. Ishwaran, pp. 34-56. Toronto: Gage.

337. Krishnan, P. and Krotki, K.J. (1976). **Growth of Alberta Families Study.** Edmonton: Population Research Laboratory, University of Alberta.

338. Larson, L.E. (1976). **The Canadian Family in Comparative Perspective.** Toronto: Prentice-Hall Canada. A textbook that emphasizes Canadian family patterns.

339. Larson, L.E. (1970). **The Family in Contemporary Society and Emerging Family Patterns.** In *Daycare: A Resource for the Contemporary Family*. Ottawa: The Vanier Institute of the Family.

340. Larson, L.E., Goltz, J.W. and Hobart, C. (1994). **Families in Canada: Social Context, Continuities, and Changes.** Toronto: Prentice-Hall Canada.

341. Meiklejohn, P., Yeager, A. and Kuch, L., eds. (1990). **Today's Family: A Critical Focus.** Toronto: Collier Macmillan. Source materials related to family life is divided into five areas of critical thought. Geared to high school students.

342. Nett, E.M. (1988). **Canadian Families: Past and Present.** Toronto: Butterworths. A historical emphasis in Canadian family life in order to understand the present structure of the family in Canada.

343. Nett, E.M. (1976). **The Changing Forms and Functions of the Canadian Family.** In *The Canadian Family*, 2nd edition, edited by K. Ishwaran. Toronto: Holt, Rinehart and Winston.

344. Norris, J.E. and Tindale, J.A. (1994). **Among Generations: The Cycle of Adult Relationships.** New York: W.H. Freeman. This book discusses the complex cycle of family relationships from generation to generation.

345. Peters, J. (1995). **Canadian Families into the Year 2000.** *International Journal of Sociology of the Family,* 25 (1), pp. 63-79.

346. Pool, D.I. and Bracher, M.D. (1974). **Aspects of Family Formation in Canada.** *Canadian Review of Sociology and Anthropology,* 11 (4), pp. 308-323.

347. Premier's Council in Support of Alberta Families (1992). **Alberta Families Today.** Edmonton.

348. Ramu, G.N. and Tavuchis, N. (1983). **Family in Canada or the Canadian Family?** In *The Canadian Family, 3rd edition,* edited by K. Ishwaran, pp. 57-67. Toronto: Gage.

349. Rubenstein, J.S. (1978). **Canada's Extended Families.** *Today in Psychiatry,* 4 (6), p. 1.

350. Schlesinger, B. (1987). **The Canadian Family: Towards the Year 2000.** *Guidance and Counselling,* 3, pp. 44-60. A summary of Canadian family trends in the 1980s.

351. Schlesinger, B. (1982). **Current Trends in the Canadian Family.** *Journal of Leisurability,* 9, pp. 9-12.

352. Schlesinger, B. (1980). **Family Life in Canada: What Will the Future Bring?** *The School Guidance Worker,* 35, pp. 28-32.

353. Schlesinger, B. (1979). **Families: Canada.** Toronto: McGraw-Hall Ryerson. An overview of family patterns in Canada.

354. Schlesinger, B. (1977). **Current Trends and Issues in Canadian Family Life.** In *Proceedings of the Regional Social Work Conference on the Canadian Military Family,* edited by B.C. Pinch and B.A. Fournier. Toronto: Canadian Forces Personnel Applied Research Unit, pp. 9-17.

355. Schlesinger, B. (1972). **Families: A Canadian Perspective.** Toronto: McGraw-Hall Ryerson. A text for high school seniors that examines Canadian family patterns in the early 1970s.

356. Schlesinger, B. and Schlesinger, R. (1992). **Canadian Families in Transition.** Toronto: Canadian Scholars' Press. This book includes changes in various patterns of Canadian families in the 1990s. The Sandwich Generation is included.

357. Schlesinger, B. and Schlesinger, R. (1988). **Families Canada: The 1980s.** *Ontario Family Studies Journal,* 7, pp. 4-10.

358. The Canadian Journal of Sociology (1981). **Canadian Families.** *Special Issue,* 6, pp. 239-388. Eight papers discuss various aspects of family life.

359. Vanier Institute of the Family (2000). **Profiling Canada's Families.** Ottawa. An extensive analysis of the trends and forces affecting Canada's families and the changes they are undergoing.

360. Vanier Institute of the Family (1993). **Canadian Families.** Ottawa. Enables readers to think about structural changes that have affected families in recent decades.

361. Vanier Institute of the Family (1992). **Canadian Families in Transition.** Ottawa. Includes family trends, challenges, principles and pathways related to the needs of families.

362. Vanier Institute of the Family (1991). **Canadian Family.** Ottawa. Data, facts, and figures related to Canadian families in booklet form.

363. Vanier Institute of the Family (1987). **Families in Transition.** *Transition,* 17, Special Issue. A summary of a conference dealing with the changing Canadian families.

364. Veevers, J.E. (1977). **The Family in Canada.** Ottawa: Statistics Canada, Profile Studies, 5, Part 3. An examination of 1971 Census data related to families.

365. Veevers, J.E. (1971). **The Family in Canada.** Volume 5, Part 3, Bulletin 5, 3-3. Catalogue 99-725. Ottawa: Statistics Canada.

366. Wargon, S. (1987). **Canada's Families in the 1980s: Crisis or Challenge?** *Transition,* 17, pp. 10-12.

367. Wargon, S. (1979). **Canadian Households and Families.** Ottawa: Statistics Canada. This survey of recent demographic trends is based on the results of Canadian census data from 1931 to 1971.

368. Whitehurst, B. (1984). **The Future of Marriage and the Nuclear Family.** In *The Family: Changing Trends in Canada,* edited by M. Baker. Toronto: McGraw-Hill Ryerson, pp. 219-232. A discussion of the future trends in Canadian family life.

369. Wylie, B.J. (1988). **All in the Family: A Survival Guide for Family Living and Loving in a Changing World.** Toronto: Key Porter. A popular digest of family relationships in Canada.

FAMILY MODELS

370. Eichler, M. (1997). **Family Shifts: Families, Policies, and Gender Equality.** Toronto: Oxford University Press. Presents models of family life in Canada.

371. Eichler, M. (1996). **The Construction of Technologically–Mediated Families.** *Journal of Comparative Studies,* 27 (2), pp. 281-308.

372. Eichler, M. (1981). **The Inadequacy of the Monolithic Model of the Family.** *The Canadian Journal of Sociology,* 6, 3, pp. 367-388. The monolithic model of the family assumes that (a) the family subserves various functions, most commonly identified as the procreative, sexual, economic, emotional, and socialization functions with a legally sanctioned context and under a condition of co-residency; (b) these functions are usually subserved concomitantly and in a congruent manner.

373. Fox, B.J. (1988). **Conceptualizing Patriarchy.** *The Canadian Review of Sociology and Anthropology,* 25, pp. 163-182. This paper examines the different meanings that feminist theorists have given to the concept of "patriarchy."

374. Glossop, R. (1992). **Family Definitions: What's it to Me?** *Transition,* pp. 5-8.

375. McDaniel, S.A. (1989). **An Alternative to the Family In Crisis Model.** In *The Family in Crisis: A Population Crisis?,* edited by J. Légaré, T.R. Balakrishnan and R.P. Beajot, pp. 439-451. Ottawa: The Royal Society of Canada.

376. Wakil, P. (1970). **On the Question of Developing a Sociology of the Canadian Family: A Methodological Statement.** *Canadian Review of Sociology and Anthropology,* 7 (2), pp. 154-157.

FAMILY: SOCIAL SERVICES

377. Baines, C., Evans, P. and Neysmith, S. (1991). **Women's Caring: Feminist Perspective on Social Welfare.** Toronto: McClelland and Stewart. This collection of papers examines the connection between caring and poverty, wife abuse, and child neglect. What are the prevailing assumptions made about care?

378. Freeman, D.S. (1985). **Social Work Practice with Families.** In *An Introduction to Social Work Practice in Canada,* edited by S.A. Yelaja. Toronto: Prentice-Hall Canada. How to work with family in a social work setting.

379. Hudson, P. and Taylor-Herley, S. (1995). **First Nations Child and Family Services, 1982–1992.** *Canadian Social Work Review,* 12 (1), pp. 72-84.

380. Irving, H. (1972). **The Family Myth.** Toronto: Copp Clark. A study of family active with a family social service agency in Toronto.

381. Mossman, M.J. (1986). **Family Law and Social Welfare in Canada.** In *Family Law and social Welfare Legislation in Canada,* edited by I. Bernier and A. Lajoie. Ottawa: Minister of Supply and Services.

382. Neysmith, S.M. (1988). **Canadian Social Services and Social Work Practice in the Field of Aging.** *Journal of Gerontological Social Work,* 12 (1/2), pp. 41-60. A good review of Canada's social services geared towards the elderly.

383. Smith, M.J. (1995). **Canadian Social Services on Behalf of the Family.** *Journal of Marriage and Family Living,* 17, pp. 208-211.

384. Turner, J.C. and Turner, F.J., eds. (1995). **Canadian Social Welfare, 3rd edition.** Toronto: Allyn and Bacon. Thirty chapters examine social welfare in Canada, which affects Canadian families.

FARM FAMILIES

385. Abell, C. and Dyck, D. (1962). **Children of Rural Families of Ontario and Prince Edward Island.** *Economic Annalist,* 32.

386. Abell, H.C. (1971). **Rural Families and Their Homes.** Waterloo: School of Urban and Regional Planning, University of Waterloo.

387. Abell, H.C. (1959). **The Farm Family in Canada.** *Econ. Annalist,* 29, pp. 53-58.

388. Abell, H.C. (1954). **The Women's Touch — in Canadian Farm Work.** *The Economic Annalist,* 24 (2), pp. 37-38.

389. Brownstone, M. (1957). **Goals and Performance Relevant to Prairie Family Farming.** *Canadian Journal of Agricultural Economics,* 4 (2), p. 94.

390. Canadian Advisory Council on the Status of Women (1987). **Growing Strong: Women in Agriculture.** Ottawa. Four papers discuss the needs of farm women. A bibliography is included.

391. Charles, E. and Anthony, S. (1943). **The Community and the Family in Prince Edward Island.** *Rural Sociology,* 7, pp. 37-51.

392. Dyck, D. (1960). **Adjustment Problems in Relocating New Brunswick Farm Families.** *Canadian Journal of Agricultural Economics,* 8 (2).

393. Dyck, D. and Lawrence, F. (1960). **Relocation Adjustments of Farm Families.** *Economic Annalist,* 30.

394. Haviland, W.E. (1958). **The Family Farm in Quebec, an Economic or Sociological Unit?** *Canadian Journal of Agricultural Economics,* 5 (2), pp. 65-88.

395. Keating, N.C. (1987). **Reducing Stress of Farm Men and Women.** *Family Relations,* 36, pp. 358-363. How farm families in Alberta can be helped in the farm crisis by family life education.

396. Kohl, B. (1978). **Women's Participation in the North American Family Farm.** *Women's Studies International Quarterly,* 1, pp. 47-54.

397. Kohl, B. (1976). **Working Together: Women and Family in Southwestern Saskatchewan.** Toronto: Holt, Rinehart and Winston.

398. McGhee, M. (1984). **Women in Rural Life.** Toronto: Ministry of Agriculture and Food. A study that examines the lives of rural women in Ontario.

399. Walker, L.S. and Walker, J.L. (1987). **Stressors and Symptoms Predictive of Distress in Farmers.** *Family Relations,* 36, pp. 374-378. A study of 808 men and women involved in farming in Manitoba.

FATHERS

400. Agbayewa, M.W. (1984). **Fathers in the Newer Family Forms: Male or Female?** *Canadian Journal of Psychiatry,* 29, pp. 402-405.

401. Dominic, K.T. and Schlesinger, B. (1980). **Weekend Fathers: Family Shadows.** *Journal of Divorce,* 3, pp. 241-247. Interviews were carried out with part-time fathers. Information was gathered about visits, the fathers' social life, financial support, and the relationship between the fathers and their children.

402. Horna, J. and Lupri, E. (1987). **Father's Participation in Work, Family Life and Leisure: A Canadian Experience.** In *Reassessing Fatherhood: New Observations on Fathers and the Modern Family,* edited by C. Lewis and M. O'Brien, eds., pp. 54-73. London: Sage.

403. Lupri, E. (1991). **Fathers in Transition: The Case of Dual-Earner Families in Canada.** In *Continuity and Change in Marriage and Family,* edited by J.E. Veevers. Toronto: Holt, Rinehart and Winston.

404. Mandell, D. (1995). **Non-Supporting Divorced Fathers: The Problem in Context.** *Canadian Social Work Review,* 12 (2), pp. 190-210.

405. Nelson, G. (1982). **Coping with the Loss of Father: Family Reaction to Death or Divorce.** *Journal of Family Issues,* 3, pp. 41-60.

406. Rosenthal, C.J. (1987). **Generational Succession: The Passing on of Family Headship.** *Journal of Comparative Family Studies,* 18, pp. 61-78. Headship of a family usually descends from father to son to grandson.

407. Rosenthal, C.J. and Marshall, V.W. (1986). **The Head of the Family: Social Meaning and Structural Variability.** *Canadian Journal of Sociology,* 11, pp. 183-198. This paper describes family headship as reported by a representative sample of adult men and women.

408. Schlesinger, B. (1978). **Single Parent Fathers: A Research Review.** *Children Today,* 7, pp. 12, 18-19, 37-39.

409. Schlesinger, B. and Dominic, K. (1980). **Weekend Fathers.** *Journal of Divorce,* 3, pp. 241-247.

410. Schlesinger, B. and Todres, R. (1976). **Motherless Families: An Increasing Societal Pattern.** *Child Welfare,* 55, pp. 553-558.

FERTILITY AND FAMILY LIFE

411. Balakrishnan, T.R., Kanter, J.K. and Allingham, J.D. (1975). **Fertility and Family Planning in a Canadian Metropolis.** Montreal: McGill-Queen's University Press.

412. Bouvier, L.F. (1968). **The Spacing of Births Among French Canadian Families: An Historical Approach.** *Canadian Review of Sociology and Anthropology,* 5 (1), pp. 17-26.

413. Eaton, J.W. and Mayer, A.J. (1953). **The Social Biology of Very High Fertility Among the Hutterites: The Demography of a Unique Population.** *Human Biology,* 25, pp. 206-264.

414. Grindstaff, C.E. (1996). **Canadian Fertility: From Boom to Bust or Stability.** *Canadian Social Trends,* pp. 12-16. A demographic analysis of various Canadian age cohorts.

415. Grindstaff, C.F. (1989). **Socio-demographic Associations with Fertility: A Profile of Canadian Women at Age 30.** *Canadian Studies in Population,* 16, pp. 43-60.

416. Grindstaff, C.F. (1984). **Catching Up: The Fertility of Women over 30 Years of Age, Canada in the 1970s and Early 1980s.** *Canadian Studies in Population,* 11, pp. 95-109.

417. Henripin, J. (1972). **Trends and Factors of Fertility in Canada, 1961 Census Monograph.** Ottawa: Statistics Canada.

418. Légaré, J. (1974). **Demographic highlights on fertility decline in Canadian marriage cohorts.** *Canadian Review of Sociology and Anthropology,* 11 (4), pp. 287-307.

419. Ram, B. (1988). **Reproduction: The Canadian Family in Transition.** *Journal of Biosocial Science,* 20, pp. 19-30.

420. Sabagh, G. (1942). **The Fertility of the French Canadian Woman during the Seventeenth Century.** *American Journal of Sociology,* 47, pp. 680-689.

421. Tepperman, L. (1974). **Ethnic Variations in Marriage and Fertility Canada, 1871.** *Canadian Review of Sociology and Anthropology,* 11 (4), pp. 324-343.

422. Wadhera, S. (1989). **Trends in Birth and Fertility Rates, Canada, 1921–1987.** *Health Reports,* 1 (2), pp. 211-223.

423. Wadhera, S. and Millar, W.J. (1991). **Patterns and Change in Canadian Fertility 1971–1988: First Births After Age 30.** *Health Reports,* 3 (2), pp. 149-161.

FRENCH–CANADIAN FAMILIES

424. Garigue, P. (1980). **French Canadian Kinship and Family Life.** In *Canadian Families: Ethnic Variations,* edited by K. Ishwaran. Toronto: McGraw-Hill Ryerson.

425. Garigue, P. (1976). **French Canadian Kinship and Urban Life.** In *The Canadian Family,* revised edition, edited by K. Ishwaran. Toronto: Holt, Rinehart and Winston. (First published in *American Anthropologist,* 58 (1956), pp. 1090-1100.

426. Garigue, P. (1971). **The French Canadian Family.** Translated by Frank E. Jones. In *Canadian Society,* abridged edition, edited by Blishen, et al., pp. 126-141. Toronto: Macmillan.

427. Garigue, P. (1965). **French Canadian Kinship and Urban Life.** In *French Canadian Society,* edited by M. Rioux and Y. Martin. Toronto: McClelland and Stewart.

428. Garigue, P. (1956). **French–Canadian Kinship and Urban Life.** *American Anthropologist,* 58, pp. 1090-1101.

429. Gerin, L. (1964). **The French–Canadian Family: Its Strengths and Weaknesses.** In *French Canadian Society,* Volume 1, edited by M. Rioux and Y. Martin. Toronto: McClelland and Stewart, pp. 32-56.

430. Gonzalve, P. (1952). **The French–Canadian Working Family.** *Canadian Welfare,* XXVIII, pp. 32-35.

431. Jean, D. (1992). **Family Allowances and Family Autonomy: Quebec Families Encounter the Welfare State, 1945–1955.** In *Canadian Family History,* edited by B. Bradbury. Toronto: Copp-Clark Pitman.

432. Miner, M. (1938). **The French Canadian Family Cycle.** *American Sociological Review,* 3, pp. 700-708.

433. Moreux, C. (1973). **The French Canadian Family.** In *Women in Canada,* edited by M. Stephenson. Toronto: General Publishing.

434. Moreaux, C. (1971). **The French–Canadian Family.** In *The Canadian Family: A Book of Readings,* edited by K. Ishwaran. Toronto: Holt, Rinehart and Winston.

435. Tremblay, M.A. (1973). **Authority Models in French Canadian Family.** In *Communities and Culture in French-Canada,* edited by G. L. Gold and M.A. Tremblay. Toronto: Holt, Rinehart and Winston

436. Verdon, M. (1980). **The Quebec Stem Family Revisited.** In *Canadian Families: Ethnic Variations,* edited by K. Ishwaran, pp. 105-124. Toronto: McGraw-Hill Ryerson.

GAY AND LESBIAN FAMILIES

437. Arnup, K., ed. (1995). **Lesbian Parenting: Living with Pride and Prejudice.** Forty papers discuss lesbian parenting in Canada.

438. Arnup, K. (1991). **We Are Family: Lesbian Mothers in Canada.** *Resources for Feminist Research,* 20 (3/4), pp. 101-107.

439. Arnup, K. (1989). **Mothers Just Like Others? Lesbians, Divorce and Child Custody in Canada.** *Canadian Journal of Women and the Law,* 3 (1), pp. 18-35.

440. Arnup, K., Geller, G., Gottlieb, A., and Wine, J., eds. (1983). **The Lesbian Issue.** *Resources for Feminine Research,* 12, Special Issue. The articles deal with various issues related to lesbians, including lesbian mothers.

441. Coalition for Lesbian and Gay Rights in Ontario (1992). **Happy Families: The Recognition of Same–Sex Spousal Relationships.** Toronto: Coalition for Lesbian and Gay Rights in Ontario.

442. Day, D. (1990). **Lesbian/Mother.** In *Lesbians in Canada,* edited by S. Stone. Toronto: Between the Lines.

443. Gay Fathers of Toronto (1981). **Gay Fathers: Some of Their Stories, Experience and Advice.** Toronto. Gay fathers write about their parenting experiences.

444. Gross, W. (1986). **Judging the Best Interests of the Child: Child Custody and the Homosexual Parent.** *Canadian Journal of Women and the Law,* 1, pp. 505-531.

445. Herman, D. (1990). **Are We Family?: Lesbian Rights and Women's Liberation.** *Osgoode Hall Law Journal,* 28 (4), pp. 789-815.

446. Nelson, F. (1996). **Lesbian Motherhood: An Exploration of Canadian Lesbian Families.** Toronto: University of Toronto Press. A study of lesbian mothers in Alberta.

447. O'Brien, C. and Weir, L. (1995). **Lesbians and Gay Men Inside and Outside Families.** In *Canadian Families: Diversity, Conflict and Change,* edited by N. Mandel and A. Duffy. Toronto: Harcourt, Brace.

448. Rayside, D. (1988). **Gay Rights and Family Values: The Passage of Bill 7 in Ontario.** *Studies in Political Economy,* 26, pp. 109-147.

449. Ryder, B. (1990). **Equality Rights and Sexual Orientation: Confronting Heterosexual Family Privilege.** *Canadian Journal of Family Law,* 9, pp. 39-97.

450. Schneider, M.S. (1988). **Often Visible: Counselling Gay and Lesbian Youth.** Toronto: Central Toronto Youth Services. The book helps the reader to understand gay and lesbian youth in Canada.

451. Stone, S.D. (1990). **Lesbians Mothers Organizing.** In *Lesbians in Canada,* edited by Sharon D. Stone. Toronto: Between the Lines.

GENDER AND FAMILY

452. Eichler, M. (1997). **Family Shifts: Families, Policies, and Gender Equity.** Toronto: Oxford University Press. The author discusses the confusing tangle of laws that define and govern families in Canada. She proposes a Social-Responsibility model of family.

453. Fox, B. (1993). **The Rise and Fall of the Breadwinner–Homemaker Family.** In *Family Patterns: Gender Relations,* edited by F. Fox. Toronto: Oxford University Press.

454. Fox, B., ed. (1980). **Hidden in the Household.** Toronto: The Women's Press.

455. Fox, B.J., ed. (1993). **Family Patterns: Gender Relations.** Toronto: Oxford University Press. A family text that features a focus on the gender relations that create families. This book has 29 chapters.

456. Greenglass, E.R. (1982). **A World of Difference: Gender Roles in Perspective.** Toronto: Wiley.

457. Luxton, M., ed. (1997). **Feminism and Families: Critical Policies and Changing Practices.** Halifax: Fernwood Publishing. Eleven chapters discuss varied aspects of Canadian family life and relate the content to a feminist perspective. Contains a very good bibliography.

458. Mackie, M. (1987). **Constructing Women and Men: Gender Socialization.** Toronto: Holt, Rinehart and Winston.

459. Mandell, N. and Duff, A., eds. (1988). **Reconstructing The Canadian Family: Feminist Perspectives.** Toronto: Butterworths. Six papers discuss selected Canadian family issues in a feminist perspective.

GRANDPARENTS

460. Gladstone, J.W. (1987). **Factors Associated with Changes in Visiting between Grandmothers and Grandchildren following an Adult Child's Marriage Breakdown.** *Canadian Journal on Aging,* 6, pp. 117-127. A discussion of face to face contact of grandmothers with their grandchildren following a child's marriage breakdown.

461. Schlesinger, B. (1984). **Grandparenthood in Canada and the United States.** Toronto: University of Toronto, Programme in Gerontology. A review of the literature on grandparenthood.

462. Schlesinger, R. and Schlesinger, B. (1999). **Grandparenthood: Multicultural Perspectives.** *Journal of Psychology and Judaism,* 22 (4), pp. 247-264.

HISTORICAL FAMILY RESEARCH

463. Abrahamson, U. (1966). **God Bless Our Home: Domestic Life in Nineteenth Century Canada.** Toronto: Burns and MacEachern Ltd.

464. Backhouse, C.B. (1992). **Married Women's Property Law in Nineteenth-Century Canada.** In *Canadian Family History: Selected Readings,* edited by B. Bradbury. Toronto: Copp-Clark Pitman.

465. Backhouse, C.B. (1991). **Petticoats and Prejudice: Women and Law in Nineteenth Century Canada.** Toronto: Women's Press.

466. Bagnell, K. (1980). **The Little Immigrants: The Orphans Who Came to Canada.** Toronto: Macmillan. Over 80,000 children were exported from Britain to the farms in Canada between 1869 and 1925. This is their story.

467. Billson, G. (1988). **The Guest Children.** Fifth House. Eleven detailed case studies of British children who were evacuated to Canada during World War II.

468. Bosher, J.F. (1975). **The Family in New France.** In S*earch for the Visible Part,* edited by B. Gough, pp. 1-13. Waterloo: Wilfrid Laurier University.

469. Bouchard, G. (1977). **Family Structures and Geographic Mobility of Laterrière, 1851–1935.** *Journal of Family History,* Winter.

470. Bradbury, B. (1993). **Working Families: Age, Gender and Daily Survival in Industrializing Montreal.** Toronto: McClelland and Stewart.

471. Bradbury, B. (1982). **The Fragmented Family: Family Strategies in the Face of Death, Illness, and Poverty, Montreal, 1860–1885.** In *Childhood and Family in Canadian Perspective,* edited by J. Parr. Toronto: McClelland and Stewart.

472. Bradbury, B. (1979). **The Family Economy and Work in an Industrializing City: Montreal in the 1870s.** In *Historical Papers,* Canadian Historical Association, pp. 71-76.

473. Bradbury, B., Gossage, P., Kolish, E. and Stewart, A. (1993). **Property and Marriage: The Law and Practice in Early Nineteenth Century Montreal.** *Histoire sociale/Social History,* XXVI, pp. 9-39.

474. Brown, J.S.H. (1980). **Strangers in Blood: Fur Trade Company Families in Indian Country.** Vancouver: University of British Columbia Press.

475. Chapman, T. (1985). **Women, Sex and Marriage in Western Canada, 1890–1920.** *Alberta History,* 33, 4, pp. 1-12.

476. Cliche, A.M. (1992). **Unwed Mothers, Families and Society during the French Regime.** In *Canadian Family History,* edited by B. Bradbury. Toronto: Copp-Clark Pitman.

477. Comacchio, C. (1993). **Nations are Built of Babies: Saving Ontario Mothers and Children, 1900–1940.** Montreal and Kingston: McGill-Queen's University Press.

478. Corbett, G.H. (1981). **Barnardo Children in Canada.** Peterborough: Woodland Publishing. The story of British children shipped to Canada and placed with families. The tragic and difficult times these children had is documented.

479. Darroch, G. and Ornstein, M. (1984). **Family and Household in Nineteenth–Century Canada: Regional Patterns and Regional Economies.** *Journal of Family History,* pp. 158-177.

480. Davitt, P., et al. (1974). **Never Done: Three Centuries of Women's Work in Canada.** Toronto: Canadian Women's Educational Press.

481. Donnelly, F.K., ed. (1986). **Family and Household in Mid–Nineteenth Century New Brunswick.** Saint John: University of New Brunswick. Seven papers discuss historical aspects of family life in New Brunswick.

482. Foulché-Delbosc, I. (1977). **Women of Three Rivers, 1651–63.** In *The Neglected Minority: Essays in Women's History*, edited by S.M. Trofemenkoff and A. Prentice. Toronto: McClelland and Stewart.

483. Gaffield, C. (1982). **Schooling, the Economy, and Rural Society in Nineteenth–Century Ontario.** In *Childhood and Family in Canadian Perspective,* edited by J. Parr. Toronto: McClelland and Stewart.

484. Gaffield, C. (1978). **Canadian Families in Cultural Context: Hypotheses from the Mid–Nineteenth Century.** *Historical Papers,* Canadian Historical Association, pp. 48-70.

485. Gagan, D. (1981). **Hopeful Travellers: Families, Land and Social Change in Mid–Victorian Peel County, Canada West.** Toronto: University of Toronto Press.

486. Gagan, D. (1976). **The prose of life–literacy reflections on the family, individual experience and social structure in nineteenth–century Canada.** *Journal of Social History,* 36, pp. 126-141.

487. Gagan, D. and Hays, H. (1973). **Historical demography and Canadian Social History: Families and Land in Peel County, Ontario.** *Canadian Historical Review,* 54, pp. 27-70.

488. Gee, E.M. (1982). **Marriage in Nineteenth–Century Canada.** *Canadian Review of Sociology and Anthropology,* 19, pp. 311-325.

489. Gee, E.M. (1980). **Female Marriage Patterns in Canada: Changes and Differentials.** *Journal of Comparative Family Studies,* 11, pp. 457-474. Analyses differentials in age at marriage and universality of marriage among Canadian women during the 1931-1976 period using Canadian census data.

490. Harrison, P., ed. (1979). **The Home Children.** Winnipeg: Watson and Dwyer. This book contains the personal stories of the children who were exported to Canada from Britain from 1869 to 1925 (80,000 children).

491. Jones, A. and Rutman, L. (1981). **For the Children's Aid: J.J. Kelso and Child Welfare in Ontario.** Toronto: University of Toronto Press.

492. Katz, M.B. (1975). **The People of Hamilton, Canada West: Family and Class in a Mid-Nineteenth Century City.** Cambridge, Mass.: Harvard University Press.

493. Kohl, B. (1971). **The Family in a Post–Frontier Society.** In *The Canadian Family,* edited by K. Ishwaran. Toronto: Holt, Rinehart and Winston.

494. Loewen, R.K. (1993). **Family, Church and Market: A Mennonite Community in the Old and the New Worlds, 1850–1930.** Toronto: University of Toronto Press.

495. Marr, W. (1986). **Nuptiality, Total Fertility and Marital Fertility in Upper Canada, 1851: A Study of Land Availability, Urbanization and Birthplace.** *Canadian Studies in Population,* 13 (1), pp. 1-18.

496. McKie, D.C., Prentice, B. and Reed, P. (1983). **Divorce: Law and the Family in Canada.** Ottawa: Minister of Supply and Services. A history of divorce and marriage in Canada since pioneering times.

497. Medjuck, S. (1979). **Family and Household Composition in the Nineteenth Century: The Case of Moncton New Brunswick 1851 to 1871.** *Canadian Journal of Sociology,* 4 (3), pp. 275-285.

498. Mishra-Bouchez, T. and Edmond, E. (1987). **The Marital Status of Gatineau Mothers Between 1976 and 1984 or the Rapid and Deep Change of a Society.** *Canadian Journal of Public Health,* 78, pp., 381-384.

499. Morrison, T.R. (1976). **"Their Proper Sphere": Feminism, The Family and Child–Centred Social Reform in Ontario, 1875–1900.** *Ontario History,* LXVIII, pp. 45-64 (pt. 1) and pp. 65-74 (pt. 2).

500. Morton, S. (1992). **The June Bride as the Working–Class Bride: Getting Married in a Halifax Working–Class Neighbourhood in the 1920s.** In *Canadian Family History,* edited by B. Bradbury. Toronto: Copp-Clark Pitman.

501. Nett, E. (1981). **Canadian Families in Socio–Historical Perspective.** *The Canadian Journal of Sociology,* 6, pp. 239-259. This paper examines historical material on Canadian families to derive a clearer understanding of Canadian society and problems faced by Canadians in the daily experiences of family life. It dispels certain myths regarding households (family structure), marriage, children, and roles of family members.

502. Parr, J., ed. (1987). **Childhood and Family in Canadian History.** Toronto: McClelland and Stewart. Eight papers discuss varied issues related to childhood and family during the 1860–1940 period.

503. Parr, J. (1980). **Labouring Children.** Montreal: McGill-Queen's University Press. Nearly 80,000 British children were apprenticed as farm labourers and domestics in Canada during the 1869–1925 period. The book looks at the lives of these children in their "new families."

504. Prentice, A. and Houston, S.E. (1975). **Family, School and Society in Nineteenth Century Canada.** Toronto: Oxford University Press.

505. Rosenfeld, M. (1988). **It Was a Hard Life: Class and Gender in the Work and Family Rhythms of a Railway Town.** In *Canadian Family History,* edited by B. Bradbury. Toronto: Copp-Clark Pitman.

506. Rowe, G. and Krishan, D. (1980). **A Comparative Analysis of Divorce Rates in Canada and the United States, 1927 to 1967.** *Journal of Divorce,* 4, pp. 61-71.

507. Snell, J. (1992). **The White Life for Two: The Defence of Marriage and Sexual Morality in Canada, 1890–1914.** In *Canadian Family History,* edited by B. Bradbury. Toronto: Copp-Clark Pitman.

508. Snell, J. (1991). **In the Shadow of the Law: Divorce in Canada, 1900–1939.** Toronto: University of Toronto Press.

509. Snell, J. (1988). **Marital Cruelty: Women and the Nova Scotia Divorce Court, 1900–1930.** *Acadiensis,* 18 (1), pp. 3-31.

510. Snell, J.G. (1990). **Filial Responsibility Laws in Canada: An Historical Study.** *Canadian Journal on Aging,* 9, pp. 268-277.

511. Strong-Boag, V. (1988). **The New Day Recalled: Lives of Girls and Women in English Canada, 1919–1939.** Toronto: Copp Clark Pitman. The contents includes childhood, paid work, courtship and marriage, domestic work, motherhood, and aging.

512. Strong-Boag, V. (1982). **Intruders in the Nursery: Child Care Professionals Reshape the Years One to Five, 1920–1940.** In *Childhood and Family in Canadian History,* edited by Joy Parr. Toronto: McClelland and Stewart, pp. 160-178.

513. Sutherland, N. (1976). **Children in English–Canadian Society.** Toronto: University of Toronto Press. An historical analysis of the lives of Canadian children in the late nineteenth century.

514. Synge, J. (1980). **Work and Family Support Patterns of the Aged in the Early Twentieth Century.** In *Aging in Canada, Social Perspectives,* edited by Victor W. Marshall. Toronto: Fitzhenry and Whiteside, pp. 135-144.

515. Urquhart, M.C. and Buckley, K.A.H., eds. (1965). **Historical Statistics of Canada.** Toronto: Macmillan of Canada.

516. Ward, P. (1990). **Courtship, Love and Marriage in Nineteenth–Century English Canada.** Montreal and Kingston: McGill-Queen's University Press.

HOUSEWIVES/HOUSEWORK

517. Brayfield, A.A. (1992). **Employment Resources and Housework in Canada.** *Journal of Marriage and the Family,* 54 (1), pp. 19-30.

518. Davies, L. and Carrier, P.J. (1999). **The Importance of Power Relations for the Division of Household Labour.** *Canadian Journal of Sociology,* 24 (1), pp. 35-51. This paper examines the division of housework in dual-earner families.

519. Duchesne, D. (1988). **The Decline of Unpaid Family Work.** *Canadian Social Trends,* 11, pp. 20-21. The unpaid family worker is a person who works without pay on a family farm or in a business or professional practice owned or operated by a related member of the same household.

520. Eichler, M. with assistance of Guppy, N. and Siltamen, J. (1977). **The Prestige of the Occupation Housewife,** in Patricia Marchak, ed. *The Working Sexes.* Vancouver: University of British Columbia: Institute for Industrial Relations, pp. 151-175.

521. Housewives in Training and Research (1986). **It's Time.** Vancouver: Housewives in Training and Research. A study of 211 housewives in the Vancouver area.

522. Kome, P. (1982). **Somebody Has to Do It: Whose Work is Housework?** Toronto: McClelland and Stewart. A survey of unpaid work that Canadian women do in the home.

523. Looker, E.D. and Thiessen, V. (1999). **Images of Work: Women's Work, Men's Work, Housework.** *The Canadian Journal of Sociology,* 24, 2, Spring, pp. 225-251. A study of 1200 seventeen year olds in Hamilton and Halifax and rural Nova Scotia about their attitudes to work.

524. Luxton, M. (1980). **More than a Labour of Love: Three Generations of Women's Work in the Home.** Toronto: The Women's Press. What life is really like for housewives.

525. Luxton, M., Rosenberg, H. and Arat-Koc, S. (1990). **Through the Kitchen Window: The Politics of Home and Family, 2nd edition.** Toronto: Garamond.

526. Proulx, M. (1978). **Five Million Women: A Study of the Canadian Housewife.** Ottawa: Advisory Council on the Status of Women. Examines the social and economic states of women who work within the house.

527. Strong-Boag, V. (1985). **Discovering the Home: The Last 150 Years of Domestic Work in Canada.** In *Women's Paid and Unpaid Work,* edited by Paula Bourne. Toronto: New Hogtown Press, pp. 35-60.

HOUSING AND FAMILY LIFE

528. Corbett, R. (1986). **The Incidence of Single Parent Families by Settlement Type in Atlantic Canada.** Nova Scotia: Mount Allison University, Dept. Of Geography. This report analyzes the housing needs of one-parent families in Atlantic Canada.

529. Klodawsky, F., Spector, A.N., and Hendrix, C. (1984). **Housing and Single Parents: An Overview of the Literature.** Toronto: Centre for Urban and Community Studies, University of Toronto. This 48 page monograph reviews the literature related to housing and single parents in Canada and the United States. There is also a 50 item annotated bibliography.

INTERMARRIAGE

530. Carisse, C. (1976). **Cultural Orientations in Marriage between French and English Canadians.** In *The Canadian Family in Comparative Perspective,* edited by Lyle E. Larsen. Scarborough: Prentice-Hall Canada.

531. Carisse, C. (1975). **Cultural Orientations in Marriages Between French and English Canadians.** In *Marriage, Family and Society: Canadian Perspectives,* edited by P. Wakil, pp. 97-112. Toronto: Butterworths.

532. Chimbos, P.D. (1971). **Immigrants' Attitudes Toward Their Children's Interethnic Marriages in a Canadian Community.** *International Migration Review,* 5, pp. 5-7.

533. Driedger, L. (1983). **Ethnic Intermarriages: Student Dating and Mating.** In *Marriage and Divorce in Canada,* edited by K. Ishwaran. Toronto: Methuen.

534. Frideres, J., Goldstein, J. and Gilbert, R. (1971). **The Impact of Jewish–Gentile Intermarriage in Canada: An Alternative View.** *Journal of Comparative Family Studies,* 2, pp. 268-275.

535. Goldstein, J. and Segall, A. (1991). **Ethnic Intermarriage and Ethnic Identity.** In *Continuity and Change in Marriage and Family,* edited by J.E. Veevers. Toronto: Holt, Rinehart and Winston of Canada.

536. Heaton, T.B. (1991). **Religious Group Characteristics, Endogamy and Interfaith Marriages.** *Social Analysis,* 51, pp. 363-376.

537. Heer, D. (1962). **The Trend of Interfaith Marriages in Canada.** *American Sociology Review,* 27, pp. 245-250.

538. Heer, D.M. and Hubey, C.A. (1976). **The Trend of Interfaith Marriages in Canada, 1922 to 1972.** In *The Canadian Family,* revised edition, edited by K. Ishwaren. Toronto: Holt, Rinehart and Winston of Canada.

539. Heer, D.M. and Hubey, C.A., Jr. (1975). **The Trend in Interfaith Marriages in Canada: 1922 to 1972.** In *Marriage, Family and Society: Canadian Perspectives,* edited by S. Parvez Wakil, pp. 85-96. Toronto: Butterworths.

540. Kalbach, W.E. (1983). **Propensities for Intermarriage in Canada as Reflected in Ethnic Origins of Husbands and their Wives 1961–1971.** In *Marriage and Divorce in Canada,* edited by K. Ishwaran. Toronto: Methuen.

541. Lambert, R.D. and Curtis, J.E. (1984). **Québécois and English Canadian Opposition to Racial and Religious Intermarriage, 1968–1983.** *Canadian Ethnic Studies,* 16, pp. 30-46.

542. Larson, L.E. and Munro, B. (1990). **Religious Intermarriage in Canada in the 1980s.** *Journal of Comparative Family Studies,* 21, pp. 239-250.

543. Larson, L.E. and Munro, B. (1985). **Religious Intermarriage in Canada, 1974–1982.** *International Journal of Sociology of the Family,* 15, pp. 31-49.

544. Rosenberg, L. (1960). **Intermarriage in Canada, 1921–1960.** In *Intermarriage and Jewish Life,* edited by M.J. Cahnman. New York: The Herzl Press.

545. Schoenfeld, S. (1987). **A Perspective on Assimilation, Intermarriage and Jewish Identity in Ontario.** Toronto: Canadian Jewish Congress, Ontario Region.

KINSHIP

546. Connidis, I. (1989). **Contact Between Siblings in Later Life.** *Canadian Journal of Sociology,* 14 (4), pp. 429-442.

547. Osterreich, H. (1965). **Geographical Mobility and Kinship: A Canadian Example.** *International Journal of Comparative Sociology,* 6 (1 and 2), pp. 131-145.

548. Paletta, A. (1992). **Today's Extended Families.** *Canadian Social Trends,* 27, pp. 26-28.

549. Piddington, R. (1973). **Kinship Network among the French–Canadians.** In *Communities and Culture in French-Canada,* edited by G.L. Gold and M. Tremblay. Toronto: Holt, Rinehart and Winston.

550. Piddington, R. (1971). **A Study of French–Canadian Kinship.** In *The Canadian Family: A Book of Readings,* edited by K. Ishwaran. Toronto: Holt, Rinehart and Winston.

551. Piddington, R. (1961). **A Study of French–Canadian Kinship.** *International Journal of Comparative Sociology,* 2 (1 and 2), pp. 3-23.

552. Pineo, P. (1969). **The Extended Family in Working Class Area of Hamilton.** In *The Canadian Society,* edited by Blishen et al., pp. 140-150. Toronto: Macmillan.

553. Pineo, P.C. (1976). **The Extended Family in a Working–Class Area of Hamilton.** In *The Canadian Family,* revised edition, edited by K. Ishwaran. Toronto: Holt, Rinehart and Winston.

554. Ramu, G.N., ed. (1979). **Kinship Networks.** In *Courtship, Marriage and the Family in Canada.* Toronto: Macmillan Company of Canada Ltd., pp. 96-114. This chapter discusses the main theoretical issues of the relationship between urbanization and kinship. It also summarizes the major findings dealing with kinship ties in urban Canada.

555. Rosenthal, C.J. (1985). **Kinkeeping in the Familial Division of Labor.** *Journal of Marriage and the Family,* 47, pp. 965-974.

556. Snider, E. (1981). **The Role of Kin in Meeting Health Care Needs of the Elderly.** *The Canadian Journal of Sociology,* 6, pp. 325-336. This article offers a brief but comprehensive review of the literature, highlighting the positive contribution of family in meeting various needs of the elderly.

LEGAL ASPECTS RELATED TO FAMILIES

557. Abella, R.S. (1981). **Economic Adjustment on Marriage Breakdown Support.** *Family Law Review,* 4 (1), pp. 1-10.

558. Abernathy, T. and Arcus, M. (1977). **The Law and Divorce in Canada.** *The Family Coordinator,* 22, pp. 409-413.

559. Bala, N. and Clarke, K.L. (1981). **The Child and the Law.** Toronto: McGraw-Hill Ryerson. A thumb-nail sketch of the Canadian laws that affect children.

560. Bala, N., Hornic, J.P. and Vogl, R., eds. (1991). **Canadian Child Welfare Law: Children, Families and the State.** Toronto: Thompson Educational Publishing.

561. Bisset-Johnson, A. and Day, D. (1986). **The New Divorce Law: A Commentary on the Divorce Act, 1985.** Toronto: Carswell.

562. Boivin, S.P. (1985). **To Marry or Not to Marry? A Study of the Legal Situation of Common Law Spouses in Canadian Law.** In *Family Law in Canada: New Directions,* edited by E. Sloss. Ottawa: Canadian Advisory Council on the Status of Women.

563. Burtch, B.E., Wachtel, A. and LaPrairie, C.P. (1985). **Marriage Preparation, Separation, Conciliation and Divorce: Findings From the Public Images of Law Study.** *Canadian Journal of Family Law,* 4, pp. 369-384.

564. Caputo, T.C. (1987). **The Young Offenders Act: Children's Rights, Children's Wrongs.** *Canadian Public Policy,* 13, pp. 125-143. An overview of juvenile justice in Canada.

565. Davies, C. (1995). **The emergence of judicial child support guidelines.** *Canadian Family Law Quarterly,* 13, pp. 89-110.

566. Department of Justice, Canada (1986). **Divorce Law for Counsellors.** Ottawa. Reviews the Divorce Act of 1985 and has a short history of divorce law in Canada (booklet).

567. Department of Justice, Canada (1986). **Divorce Law: Questions and Answers.** Ottawa: Department of Justice. A booklet that clarifies the divorce law as of June 1, 1986.

568. Foote, C. (1984). **The Legislation on Spousal and Child Support at Separation and Divorce: An Analysis of the Principles Behind the Law.** Toronto: Dept. of Sociology in Education, Ontario Institute for Studies in Education. This paper reviews the available research data on support in Canada and the relevant federal and Ontario legislation.

569. Foote, C.E. (1987). **Recent State Responses to Separation and Divorce in Canada: Implications for Families and Social Welfare.** *Canadian Social Work Review,* 5, pp. 28-43. A discussion of Canadian laws affecting separation and divorce.

570. Irving, H., ed. (1981). **Family Law: An Interdisciplinary Perspective.** Toronto: Carswell. Eight papers discuss various aspects related to family law in Canada. Included in the topics are conciliation counselling, joint custody, child abuse and the court system.

571. Jamieson, K. (1978). **Indian Women and the Law in Canada.** Ottawa: Canadian Advisory Council on the Status of Women.

572. Kronby, M.C. (1991). **Canadian Family Law, 5th edition.** Don Mills: Stoddard.

573. Langford, J.S. (1982). **The Law of Your Land.** Toronto: Canadian Broadcasting Corporation. A practical guide to the new Canadian Constitution. Family law is included in this booklet.

574. Mendes da Costa, D. (1978). **Domestic Contracts in Ontario.** *Canadian Journal of Family Law,* 1, pp. 232-253.

575. Menear, M.A. (1995). **Effectiveness of domestic contracts.** *Canadian Family Law Quarterly,* 13, pp. 1-24.

576. Ministry of the Attorney General (1987). **Marriage as an Equal Partnership: A Guide to the Family Law Act.** Toronto. This booklet discusses the reforms contained in the Family Law Act of 1986 in Ontario.

577. Ministry of the Attorney General (1984). **Where Do I Stand? A Child's Legal Guide to Separation and Divorce.** Toronto.

578. Mohr, J.W. (1984). **The Future of the Family, the Law and the State.** *Canadian Journal of Family Law,* 4, pp. 261-273.

579. Morton, M.E. (1988). **Dividing the Wealth, Sharing the Poverty: the (re)formation of family law in Ontario.** *Canadian Review of Sociology and Anthropology,* 2, pp. 254-275. A critical feminist analysis of the changes in the family law of Ontario.

580. Ontario Law Reform Commission (1993). **Report on the Rights and Responsibilities of Cohabitants Under the Family Law Act.** Toronto: Ministry of the Attorney General.

581. Pask, E.D. (1993). **Family Law and Policy in Canada: Economic Implications for Single Custodial Mothers and their Children.** In *Single Parent Families,* edited by J. Hudson and B. Gallaway. Toronto: Thompson Educational Publishing.

582. Thomlison, R.J. and Foote, C.E. (1987). **Children and the Law in Canada: The Shifting Balance of Children's, Parents', and the State's Rights.** *Journal of Comparative Family Studies,* 18, pp. 207-230. Outlines the important principles that underlie the legislation and that reflect the continuing attempt to balance conflicting rights.

583. Vayda, E.J. and Satterfield, M.T. (1984). **Law for Social Workers: A Canadian Guide.** Toronto: Carswell. A primer of family law for social workers.

584. Wolfson, L.H. (1987). **The New Family Law.** Toronto: Random House. Examines Ontario's 1986 Family Law Act. It critically looks at the new changes in the legislation.

MARRIAGE

585. Aubé, N. and Linden, W. (1991). **Marital Disturbance, Quality of Communication and Socioeconomic Status.** *Canadian Journal of Behavioural Science,* 23, pp. 125-132.

586. Bartoletti, M. and Bartoletti, L. (1985). **Courtship in Canada.** Toronto: Guidance Centre, Faculty of Education, University of Toronto. This booklet discusses courtship in Canada.

587. Campbell, D.F. and Neice, D.C. (1979). **The Ties that Bind — Structure and Marriage in Nova Scotia.** Port Credit: The Scribbler's Press.

588. Cheal, D. (1983). **Changing Household Financial Strategies: Canadian Couples Today.** *Human Ecology,* 21 (2), pp. 197-213.

589. Cohn, W. (1976). **Jewish Outmarriage and Anomie: A Study in the Canadian Syndrome of Polarities.** *Canadian Review of Sociology and Anthropology,* 13, pp. 90-105.

590. de Ruyter, B. (1976). **Ethnic Differentials in Age at First Marriage, Canada, 1971.** *Journal of Comparative Family Studies,* 7, pp. 159-166.

591. den Boggende, B. (1987). **A Historical Survey of the Rite of Marriage: Pre–Christian and Christian.** *Grail,* 3, pp. 59-78. The origin, development, and conflict of three models of marriage.

592. Gee, E.M.T. and Ellen, M. (1982). **Marriage in Nineteenth–Century Canada.** *Canadian Review of Sociology and Anthropology,* 19, pp. 311-325. Census data for the period 1851–1891 are examined.

593. Glossop, R. (1993). **Canadian Marriage and Family: Future Directions.** In *Marriage and the Family in Canada Today,* 2nd edition, edited by G.N. Ramu, Chapter 12. Toronto: Prentice-Hall Canada,

594. Goltz, J.W. and Larson, L.E. (1991). **Religiosity, Marital Commitment and Individualism.** *Family Perspective,* 25, pp. 201-219.

595. Grindstaff, C.F. (1988). **Adolescent Marriage and Childbearing: The Long Term Economic Outcome, Canada in the 1980s.** *Adolescence,* 33, pp. 45-58.

596. Guldner, C.A. (1987). **The Future of Christian Marriage.** *Grail,* 3, pp. 47-58. A review of modern marriage in a Christian context.

597. Hobart, C. (1973). **Equalitarianism After Marriage.** In *Women in Canada,* edited by Marylee Stephenson, pp. 138-156. Toronto: New Press.

598. Hobart, C. (1972). **Orientations to Marriage Among Young Canadians.** *Journal of Comparative Family Studies,* 3, pp. 171-193.

599. Hobart, C.W. (1975). **Ownership of Matrimonial Property: A Study of Practices and Attitudes.** *Canadian Review of Sociology and Anthropology,* 12 (4), Part I, pp. 440-452.

600. Kurian, G. (1993). **Marital Patterns in Canada.** In *Marriage and the Family in Canada Today,* 2nd edition, edited by G.N. Ramu. Toronto: Prentice-Hall Canada.

601. Larson, L.E. (1984). **Marital Breakdown in Canada: A Sociological Analysis?** In *Christian Marriage Today. Growth or Breakdown? Interdisciplinary Essays,* edited by J. A. Buijs. New York: The Edwin Mellen Press, pp. 35-69.

602. Lupri, E. and Frideres, J. (1981). **The Quality of Marriage and the Passage of Time: Marital Satisfaction Over the Family Life Cycle.** *Canadian Journal of Sociology,* 6, pp. 283-305. This article examines the effect of the passage of time on the quality of marriage.

603. MacDougall, D.J. (1995). **Marriage Resolution and Recognition in Canada.** *Family Law Quarterly,* 29, pp. 541-548.

604. Nagnur, D. and Adams, O. (1987). **Tying the Knot: An Overview of Marriage Rates in Canada.** *Canadian Social Trends,* pp. 2-6. A statistical analysis of marriage and remarriage in Canada, 1931–85.

605. Nett, E. (1978). **A Research Note: On Reviewing the Canadian Literature on Marital Interaction, 1967–1977.** *Journal of Comparative Family Studies,* 9, pp. 373-383.

606. Nett, E.M. (1979). **Marriage and the Family: Organization and Interaction.** In *Courtship, Marriage and the Family in Canada,* edited by G.N. Ramu. Toronto: Macmillan Company of Canada Limited, pp. 59-77. This chapter describes the roles played by wives and husbands to locate sources of consensus and conflict in marriage, to indicate the effect of marital negotiations in the family and the persons in marriage, and to discus marital adjustment.

607. Oderkirk, J. (1994). **Marriage in Canada: Changing Beliefs and Behaviours: 1600–1990.** *Canadian Social Trends,* pp. 2-7.

608. Palmer, S.E. (1971). **Reasons for Marriage Breakdown: A Case Study in South–Western Ontario.** *Journal of Comparative Family Studies,* 2, pp. 251-262.

609. Pineo, P.C. (1976). **Disenchantment in the Later Years of Marriage.** *Marriage and Family Living,* 23, pp. 3-11.

610. Ramu, G.N., ed. (1979). **Courtship, Marriage, and the Family in Canada: An Overview.** In *Courtship, Marriage, and the Family in Canada.* Toronto: Macmillan

Company of Canada Limited, pp. 180-195. The author states that there are two conflicting ideologies in relation to mate selection.

611. Rhyne, D. (1981). **Bases of Marital Satisfaction Among Men and Women.** *Journal of Marriage and the Family,* 43, pp. 941-955.

612. Robinson, B.W. and McVey, W.W. Jr. (1985). **The Relative Contributions of Death and Divorce to Marital Dissolution in Canada and the United States.** *Journal of Comparative Family Studies,* 16, pp. 93-110. An analysis of selected aspects of marriage dissolution by death and divorce in Canada. Since the 1960s, divorce has replaced death as a dissolution of marriages.

613. Schlesinger, B. (1980). **Trends in Marriage and the Family of the 1980s: A Canadian Viewpoint.** *The Family Life Educator,* 10, pp. 5-6.

614. Schlesinger, B., ed. (1975). **The Chatelaine Guide to Marriage.** Toronto: Macmillan. A selected number of articles dealing with marriage in Canada and printed in *Chatelaine.*

615. Trovato, F. (1988). **A Macro–Sociological Analysis of Change in the Marriage Rate: Canadian Women, 1921–25 to 1981–85.** *Journal of Marriage and the Family, 50, pp. 507-521.* An analysis of changing marriage rates. In the 1980s Canadian women marry less frequently and at a later age.

616. Wakil, S.P. (1976). **Marriage and Family in Canada.** *Journal of Comparative Family Studies,* Calgary. An overview of demographic and cultural processes related to marriage and the family in Canada.

617. Wakil, S.P. and Wakil, E.A. (1976). **Marriage and Family in Canada: A Demographic–Cultural Profile.** In *The Canadian Family,* edited by K. Ishwaran. Toronto: Holt, Rinehart and Winston of Canada.

618. White, J.M. (1987). **Marital Perceived Agreement and Actual Agreement over the Family Life Cycle.** *Journal of Comparative Family Studies,* 18, pp. 47-60. As the number of children increases in the family, so does the actual agreement between husband and wife.

MENTAL HEALTH AND FAMILY LIFE

619. Abosh, B. and Collins, A., eds. (1996). **Mental Illness in the Family: Issues and Trends.** Toronto: University of Toronto Press. Twelve papers, and 14 Canadian experts discuss mental illness and family life.

620. Ackerman, R.J., ed. (1986). **Growing in the Shadow: Children of Alcoholics.** Toronto: Addiction Research Foundation. Various authors give insights, opinions, and perspectives on the topic of children of alcoholics.

621. Canadian Journal of Community Mental Health (1986). **Women and Mental Health.** *Special Issue,* 5. Eight papers discuss various aspects of Canadian women and their mental health.

622. Cork, R.M. (1969). **The Forgotten Children.** Toronto: Addiction Research Foundation. A study of children aged 10–16 years who were living in homes of alcoholics.

623. Huddleston, R.J. and Hawkins, L. (1991). **A Comparison of Physical and Emotional Health After Divorce in a Canadian and United States Sample.** *Journal of Divorce and Remarriage,* 15, pp. 193-207.

624. Morrison, W., Page, G., Sehl, M. and Smith, H. (1986). **Single Mothers in Canada: An Analysis.** *Canadian Journal of Community Mental Health,* 5, pp. 34-48. Areas of concern covered in this paper include role strain, poverty, employment, and child care.

625. Wesley, W.A. and Epstein, N.B. (1969). **The Silent Majority.** San Francisco: Jossy Bass. A study of non-clinical families in Montreal.

626. White, J.M. (1992). **Marital Status and Well-Being in Canada: An Analysis of Age Group Variations.** *Journal of Family Issues,* 13, pp. 390-409.

MILITARY/FOREIGN SERVICE AND FAMILY LIFE

627. Foreign Service Community Association (1980). **Selected Papers on Mobility and the Family in the Canadian Foreign Service.** Ottawa: Foreign Service Committee. Eight papers discuss the problems faced by the Canadian foreign service family.

628. Harrison, D. and Laliberté, L. (1994). **No Life Like It: Military Wives in Canada.** Toronto: James Lorimer & Co. A study of 150 military wives, about family life in the Canadian military.

629. Pinch, F.C. and Fournier, B.A., eds. (1977). **Proceedings of the Regional Social Conference on the Canadian Military Family.** Toronto: Canadian Forces Personnel Applied Research Unit. The proceedings of a conference that dealt with various family issues affecting the Canadian Forces.

630. Schlesinger, B. (1978). **The Military Family in Canada: Some Issues.** *The Social Worker,* 46, pp. 36-42.

NON–TRADITIONAL FAMILIES

631. Burke, M.A. (1986). **Families: Diversity the New Norm.** *Canadian Social Trends,* 1, pp. 6-10.

632. Marcil-Gratton, N. (1989). **Growing Up Within a Family: Canadian Children and Their Parents' New Lifestyles.** *Transition,* 19, pp. 4-7.

633. Schlesinger, B. and Marshall, D. (1978). **Communal Family Living: A Canadian Alternative.** *Social Science,* 53, pp. 217-219.

634. Whitehurst, R.N. (1979). **Non–Traditional Family and Marriage.** In *Courtship, Marriage and the Family in Canada,* edited by G.N. Ramu. Toronto: Macmillan of Canada, pp. 166-179. A discussion of alternate family life styles.

635. Whitehurst, R.N. (1975). **Alternate Life Styles and Canadian Pluralism.** In *Marriage, Family and Society,* edited by P. Wakil, pp. 432-445. Toronto: Butterworths.

636. Wilson, S. (1984). **Nontraditional Living Arrangements.** In *The Family: Changing Trends in Canada,* edited by M. Baker. Toronto: McGraw-Hill Ryerson, pp. 198-218. A short examination of non-traditional family forms of living in Canada.

ONE PARENT FAMILIES: OVERVIEW

637. Davids, L. (1985). **The Lone–Parent Family in Canada: The Quantitative 1985 Backgrounds.** In *The One Parent Family in the 1980s,* edited by B. Schlesinger. Toronto: University of Toronto Press.

638. Eichler, M. (1993). **Lone Parent Families: An Instable Category in Search of Stable Policies.** In *Single Parent Families: Perspectives on Research and Policy,* edited by J. Hudson and B. Galaway. Toronto: Thompson Educational Publishing.

639. Ercul, D., Goldenberg, N. and Schlesinger, B. (1979). **Children in One–Parent Families.** In *One in Ten: The Single Parent in Canada,* edited by B. Schlesinger, pp. 16-20, Toronto: OISE Press.

640. Fels, L. and Girling, Z. (1986). **Suddenly Single: A Guide for Recently Widowed, Separated, or Divorced Women.** Toronto: YWCA. A handbook to help women who have suddenly become single parents.

641. Guyatt, D.E. (1971). **One–Parent Family in Canada.** Ottawa: Vanier Institute of the Family.

642. Hudson, J. and Galaway, B., eds. (1993). **Single Parent Families: Perspectives on Research and Policy.** Toronto: Thomson Educational Publishing. An examination of the situation of Canadian one-parent families by a group of academics.

643. Hurley, D., ed. (1987). **Separation, Divorce, Remarriage: Social, Psychological and Legal Perspectives.** London: King's College.

644. Lero, D.S. and Brockman, L.M. (1993). **Single Parent Families in Canada: A Closer Look.** In *Single Parent Families: Perspectives on Research and Policy,* edited by J. Hudson and B. Galaway. Toronto: Thompson Educational Publishing.

645. Li, S. (1978). **Options for Single Mothers.** Toronto: Social Planning Council of Metropolitan Toronto, Project Child Care, Working Paper #4. An examination of working single-parent mothers in Toronto.

646. Maureen, M. (1989). **Female Lone Parenting over the Life Course.** *Canadian Journal of Sociology,* 14 (3), pp. 335-352.

647. Moore, M. (1991). **How Long Alone? The Duration of Female Lone Parenthood in Canada.** In *Continuity and Change in Marriage and Family,* edited by Jean E. Veevers. Toronto: Holt, Rinehart and Winston.

648. Moore, M. (1989). **Female Lone Parenting Over the Life Course.** *Canadian Journal of Sociology,* 14, pp. 335-351.

649. Moore, M. (1989). **How Long Alone? The Duration of Female Lone Parenthood in Canada.** *Transition,* pp. 4-5.

650. Moore, M. (1988). **Female Lone Parenthood: The Duration of Episodes.** *Canadian Social Trends,* pp., 40-42. A statistical analysis of how long women remain lone parents in Canada.

651. Moore, M. (1987). **Women Parenting Alone.** *Canadian Social Trends,* pp. 31-36. A summary of the lives of female lone parents in Canada in 1986.

652. Morton, S. (1992). **Women on their Own: Single Mothers in Working Class Halifax.** *Acadiensis,* 19 (2), pp. 90-107.

653. Parsons, M.D. (1990). **Lone Parent Canadian Families and the Socioeconomic Achievements of Children as Adults.** *Journal of Comparative Family Studies,* 21, pp. 353-367.

654. Pool, I. and Moore, M. (1986). **Lone Parenthood: Characteristics and Determinants.** Ottawa: Supply and Services Canada.

655. Schlesinger, B. (1996). **Jewish Canadian Female–Headed One–Parent Families.** In *Change and Impact: Essays in Canadian Social Sciences,* edited by S.F. Zerker. Jerusalem: The Magnes Press, pp. 281-303.

656. Schlesinger, B., ed. (1988). **Daddy's Gone: A Study of Jewish Single Mothers in Toronto.** Toronto: Jewish Family and Child Service of Metropolitan Toronto. The findings of a study that interviewed 55 mothers who were heading one-parent families. This booklet highlights the results of the study.

657. Schlesinger, B. (1983). **Living in One–Parent Families: The Children's Perspective.** In *The Canadian Family,* edited by K. Ishwaran. Toronto: Gage, pp. 331-339.

658. Schlesinger, B. (1982). **Children's Viewpoints of Living in a One–Parent Family.** *Journal of Divorce,* 5, pp. 1-23.

659. Schlesinger, B. (1982). **One–Parent Families — Children's Viewpoint.** *Education Manitoba,* 8, pp. 4-10. Children from one-parent families were interviewed. This involved open-ended questions. The average age of the children was 14.87 and the average length of time they had been living in a single-parent family was 4.7 years.

660. Schlesinger, B. (1980). **Children in One–Parent Families in Canada: 1976.** *Journal (Ontario C.A.S.),* 23, pp. 10-12.

661. Schlesinger, B. (1980). **One–Parent Families and their Children in Canadian Society.** In *the Family and the Socialization of Children.* Ottawa: Social Sciences and Humanities Research Council of Canada, pp. 82-114.

662. Schlesinger, B. (1979). **One in Ten: One–Parent Families in Canada.** Toronto: Guidance Centre, Faculty of Education, University of Toronto.

663. Schlesinger, B. and Todres, R. (1979). **Characteristics of Canadian Members of Parents Without Partners.** In *One in Ten: The Single Parent in Canada,* edited by B. Schlesinger. Toronto: Guidance Centre, Faculty of Education, University of Toronto, pp. 107-111. This study looked at the nature of the

members of P.W.P. in Canada in 1974. Questionnaires were sent to members of P.W.P. throughout Canada. The response rate was 13 percent.

664. Todres, R. (1979). **Motherless Families and Deserting Wives.** In *One in Ten: The Single Parent in Canada,* edited by B. Schlesinger. Toronto: Guidance Centre, Faculty of Education, University of Toronto, pp. 8-15. The number of motherless homes has increased in Canada in recent years (40 percent between 1966 and 1971, and 20 percent between 1970 and 1973). The two studies reported here responded to the lack of research on this phenomenon.

665. Wargon, S. (1987). **Canada's Lone–Parent Families.** Catalogue 99-933. Ottawa: Department of Supply and Services, Statistics Canada.

ONE PARENT FAMILIES: NON–MARRIED PARENTS

666. Belle, M. and McQuillan, K. (1994). **Births outside marriage: A growing alternative.** *Canadian Social Trends,* pp. 14-17.

667. Borowski, H. and Macdonald, J.G. (1982). **The Adolescent Mother and Her Child: Issues and Trends.** Toronto: Faculty of Social Work, University of Toronto. A review of existing studies related to teenage mothers.

668. Davies, L. and McAlpine, D.D. (1998). **The Significance of Family, Work and Power Relations for Mothers' Mental Health.** *Canadian Journal of Sociology,* 23 (4), pp. 369-387.

669. Lightman, E. and Schlesinger, B. (1982). **Pregnant Adolescents in Maternity Homes: Some Professional Concerns.** In *Pregnancy in Adolescence,* edited by I.B. Stuart and C.F. Wells. New York: Van Nostrand Reinhold, pp. 363-385. A study of pregnant teenagers who were living in a maternity home in Toronto.

670. Little, M. (1994). **Manhunts and Bingo Blabs: The Moral Regulation of Ontario Single Mothers.** *Canadian Journal of Sociology,* 19.

671. Macdonnell, S. (1981). **Vulnerable Mothers, Vulnerable Children.** Halifax: Nova Scotia, Dept. of Social Services. A follow-up study of 353 non-married mothers who kept their children.

672. Mackay, H. and Austin, C. (1983). **Single Adolescent Mothers in Ontario.** Ottawa: The Canadian Council on Social Development. A study of 87 single adolescent mothers in various parts of Ontario.

673. Sacks, D., Macdonald, J.G., Schlesinger, B. and Lambert, C. (1982). **The Adolescent Mother and Her Child: A Research Study.** Toronto: Faculty of Social Work, University of Toronto. A study of 50 teenage mothers in Toronto.

674. Schlesinger, B. (1985). **The Single Teen–age Canadian Mother in the 1980s: A Review.** In *The One-Parent Family in the 1980s,* edited by B. Schlesinger. Toronto: University of Toronto Press, pp. 35-56.

675. Schlesinger, B. (1979). **The Unmarried Mother Who Keeps Her Child.** In *One in Ten: The Single Parent in Canada,* edited by B. Schlesinger. Toronto: Guidance Centre, Faculty of Education, University of Toronto, pp. 77-86. The number of children born to single mothers in Canada in 1973 was 31,005, which made up nine percent of the live births in that year. Approximately 80 percent of these children were kept by their natural mother.

ONE PARENT FAMILIES: SEPARATION

676. Ambert, A.M. (1983). **Separated Women and Remarriage Behavior: A Comparison of Financially Secure Women and Financially Insecure Women.** *Journal of Divorce,* 6, pp. 43-54.

677. Arnold, R., Wheeler, M., and Pendrith, F. (1980). **Separation and After: A Research Report.** Toronto: Ministry of Community and Social Services. The study was largely exploratory in intent. It was based on a conception of separation as a fundamental "status passage," involving changes in mental health, in relations with other family members, in dealing with friends and in relations with the broader community.

678. Baker, M. (1984). **Women Helping Women: The Transition from Separation to Divorce.** *Conciliation Courts Review,* 22 (1), pp. 53-63.

679. Boyd, M. (1977). **The Forgotten Minority: The Socioeconomic Status of Divorced and Separated Women.** In *The Working Sexes,* edited by Patricia Marchak. Vancouver: University of British Columbia, pp. 47-71.

680. Cook, D. (1979). **Separation and Divorce in Canada** *Canadian Journal of Public Health,* 70 (4), pp. 271-275.

681. Gibson, N. (1986). **Separation and Divorce: A Canadian Woman's Survival Guide.** Edmonton: Hurtig Publishers. This book gives advice on how to get through the streets of separation and divorce, including legal advice.

682. Health and Welfare Canada (1985). **The Child of the Broken Family.** Ottawa. The proceedings of a national symposium of services for children affected by separation and divorce.

683. McKenzie, B. and Guberman, I. (1997). **For the Sake of Children: A Program for Separating and Divorced Parents.** *The Social Worker,* 65, 3, pp. 107-118.

684. McVey, W.W., Jr. and Robinson, B.W. (1981). **Separation in Canada: New Insights Concerning Marital Dissolution.** *Canadian Journal of Sociology,* 6, pp. 353-366. The authors of this paper question the validity of divorce statistics as an adequate indicator of marital disruption in Canada.

685. Robertson, H. (1974). **Salt of the Earth.** Toronto: James Lorimer & Co.. Deserted women homesteading in the Prairies.

ONE PARENT FAMILIES: WIDOWS/WIDOWERS

686. Martin-Matthews, A. (1987). **Support Systems of Widows in Canada.** In *Widows: Volume II,* edited by H.Z. Lopata. Durham: Duke University Press.

687. Martin-Matthews, A. (1987). **Widowhood as an Expectable Life Event.** In *Aging in Canada: Social Perspectives,* 2nd edition, edited by V.W. Marshall. Marham: Fitzhenry and Whiteside.

688. Matthews, A. (1982). **Canadian Research on Women as Widows: A Comparative Analysis of the State of the Art.** *Resources for Feminist Research,* 11, pp. 227-230.

689. Matthews, A. (1980). **Women and Widowhood.** In *Aging in Canada: Social Perspectives,* edited by Victor W. Marshall, pp. 145-153. Toronto: Fitzhenry and Whiteside. This paper examines the state of widowhood in Canada particularly as it affects not only women's identity and concept of self, but also social roles and family relationships.

690. McLean, L. (1991). **Single Again: Widow's Work in the Urban Family Economy, Ottawa, 1871.** *Ontario History,* 83 (2), pp. 127-150.

691. Northcott, H.C. (1984). **Widowhood and Remarriage Trends in Canada 1956 to 1981.** *Canadian Journal on Aging,* 3, pp. 63-78.

692. Schlesinger, B. (1979). **Widows and Widowers as Single Parents.** In *One in Ten: The Single Parent in Canada,* edited by B. Schlesinger. Toronto: Guidance Centre, Faculty of Education, University of Toronto, pp. 37-45. There are 213,657 widowed families in Canada. Forty-seven percent of these families are headed by

a person under 55 years; 247,000 children are affected, 50 percent of them under 14 years.

693. Schlesinger, B. (1971). **The Widows and Widower in Remarriage.** *Omega,* 2, pp. 10-18.

694. Schlesinger, B. (1971). **The Widowed as a One–Parent Family Unit.** *Social Science,* pp. 26-32.

695. Simon Fraser University (1999). **Facing Widowhood: A Practical Guide.** Vancouver: Gerontology Research Centre. A booklet to help women and men during the first year after the death of a spouse.

696. Vachon, M.L.S. (1976). **Grief and Bereavement Following the Death of a Spouse.** *Canadian Psychiatric Association Journal,* 21, pp. 35-44.

697. Wu, Z. (1995). **Remarriage after Widowhood: A marital history study of older Canadians.** *Canadian Journal on Aging,* 14, pp. 719-736.

POSTPONED PARENTHOOD

698. Schlesinger, B. (1989). **Postponed Parenthood: Trends and Issues.** *Journal of Comparative Family Studies,* 20 (3), pp. 355-363.

699. Schlesinger, B. (1987). **Postponed Parenthood: A Canadian Study.** *Conciliation Courts Review,* 23, pp. 21-26.

700. Schlesinger, B. and Giblon, S.T. (1985). **Postponed Parenthood.** Toronto: Guidance Centre, Faculty of Education, University of Toronto. This booklet reviews the literature related to postponed parenthood and reports the findings of a study of Canadian couples who delayed chilldrearing.

701. Schlesinger, B. and Schlesinger, R. (1989). **Postponed Parenthood: Trends and Issues.** *Journal of Comparative Family Studies,* 20, pp. 355-363.

702. Schlesinger, B., Danaher, A. and Roberts, C. (1984). **Dual Career, Delayed Childbearing Families: Some Observations.** *Canada's Mental Health,* 32, pp. 4-6. A discussion of postponed parenthood in Canada. Case illustrations are included.

POVERTY AND FAMILY LIFE

703. Canadian Child Welfare Association (1988). **A Choice of Futures: Canada's Commitment to its Children.** Ottawa. This booklet outlines the situation of poverty among Canada's children. More than one million children in 1986 were growing up in poverty.

704. Dooley, M.D. (1991). **The Demography of Child Poverty in Canada, 1973–1986.** *Canadian Studies in Population,* 18, pp. 53-74.

705. Economic Council of Canada (1992). **The New Face of Poverty, Income Security Needs of Canadian Families.** Catalogue EC22-186/1992E. Ottawa: Supply and Services Canada.

706. National Council of Welfare (1988). **Poverty Profile.** Ottawa. A comprehensive analysis of poverty in Canada in 1986, including family poverty.

707. Ross, D. (1994). **The Canadian Factbook on Poverty.** Ottawa: Canadian Council on Social Development.

708. Ross, D., co-ordinator (1984). **Not Enough: The Meaning and Measurement of Poverty in Canada.** Ottawa: Canadian Council on Social Development. Detailed information related to the extent, depth, and length of poverty in Canada.

709. Schlesinger, B. (1982). **What About Poverty in Canada, 2nd edition.** Toronto: Guidance Centre, Faculty of Education, University of Toronto. This booklet discusses how poverty affects Canadian families.

710. Vanier Institute of the Family (1988). **Child Poverty: A National Priority?** *Transition,* 18. Various articles discuss child poverty in Canada. The latest statistical trends are included.

REMARRIAGE/STEPFAMILIES

711. Ambert, A.M. (1986). **Being a Step–Parent: Live–In and Visiting Step–Children.** *Journal of Marriage and the Family,* 48, pp. 795-804.

712. Brown, D. and Hobart, C. (1988). **Effects of Prior Marriage Children on Adjustment in Remarriage: A Canadian Study.** *Journal of Comparative Family Studies,* 19, pp. 381-396.

713. Burch, T.K. (1990). **Remarriage of Older Canadians.** *Research on Aging,* 12, pp. 546-559.

714. Clubb, A.N. (1988). **Love in the Blended Family.** Toronto: N.C. Press Ltd. As a second wife and stepmother the author discusses life in a stepfamily.

715. Davids, L. (1982). **Divorce and Remarriage Among Canadian Jews.** *Journal of Comparative Family Studies,* 13, pp. 37-47. The traditional self-image of the Jews and their culture includes the belief that Jewish family life is stable and happy. It would be expected that divorce rates as a result would be lower among Jews than Canadians in general. Traditionally, divorce among this group was legitimate but regarded as a tragedy.

716. Gross, P. (1987). **Defining Post–Divorce Remarriage Families: A Typology Based on the Subjective Perceptions of Children.** *Journal of Divorce,* 10, pp. 205-217. Reports on a Canadian study of stepfamilies.

717. Hobart, C. (1991). **Conflict in Remarriages.** *Journal of Divorce and Remarriage,* 15, pp. 69-85.

718. Hobart, C. (1988). **Relationships in Remarried Families.** *Canadian Journal of Sociology,* 13 (3), pp. 261-282. A study of husbands and wives in 232 remarried families in a large Canadian city in 1984.

719. Hobart, C. (1988). **The Family System in Remarriage: An Exploratory Study.** *Journal of Marriage and the Family,* 50, pp. 649-662. A study of 232 remarried and 102 first-married families. The investigation examined interpersonal relationships in remarried families in Alberta.

720. Hobart, C. and Brown, D. (1988). **Effects of Prior Marriage Children on Adjustment in Remarriage: A Canadian Study.** *Journal of Comparative Family Studies,* 29, pp. 381-396. Interviews were held of 232 remarried and 102 first married families. The differences in relationships of the children were examined.

721. Kuzel, P. and Krishnan, P. (1973). **Changing Patterns of Remarriage in Canada, 1961–1966.** *Journal of Comparative Family Studies,* 4 (2), pp. 215-224.

722. Messinger, L. (1984). **Remarriage: A Family Affair.** New York: Plenum Press. A comprehensive discussion of remarriage by one of Canada's pioneers in working with remarried families.

723. Messinger, L. (1976). **Remarriages Between Divorced People and Children from Previous Marriages: A Proposal for Preparation for Remarriage.** *Journal of Marriage and Family Counseling,* 2, pp. 193-200.

724. Messinger, L. and Walker, K. (1981). **From Marriage Breakdown to Remarriage: Parental Tasks and Therapeutic Guidelines.** *American Journal of Orthopsychiatry,* 51, pp. 429-438. The size of sample: 200 questionnaires to

divorced, remarried couples between the ages of 20–40 and 70 interviews (in Toronto).

725. Messinger, L., Walker, K. and Freeman, S. (1978). **Preparation for Remarriage Following Divorce.** *American Journal of Orthopsychiatry, 48,* pp. 263-272. This article is a summary of the experience of the authors who ran four weekly group meetings with 22 couples in Toronto in which at least one partner had children from a previous marriage. The experience offered (1) societal support; (2) factual information; and (3) opportunity for emotional interaction.

726. Morrison, K. and Thompson-Guppy, A. (1986). **Stepmothers Exploring the Myth.** Ottawa: Council on Social Development. The challenges, problems, and rewards of stepmothering are discussed.

727. Paris, E. (1984). **Stepfamilies: Making Them Work.** Toronto: Avon Books. Effective advice for stepfamilies by a stepmother.

728. Peters, J.F. (1976). **A Comparison of Mate Selection and Marriage in the First and Second Marriages.** *Journal of Comparative Family Studies,* 7 (3), pp. 483-490.

729. Roberts, J.R. (1988). **Divorce and Remarriage in the Modern Roman Catholic Context.** *Grail,* 4, pp. 7-30. An extensive review of the present issue of divorce and remarriage in the Catholic tradition in Canada.

730. Schlesinger, B. (1983). **Remarriage in Canada: An Overview.** *Journal (Ontario C.A.S.),* 27, pp. 5-8.

731. Schlesinger, B. (1981). **Remarriage in America and Canada: An Overview of the Literature, 1943–1960.** *Conciliation Courts Review,* 19, pp. 21-36.

732. Schlesinger, B. (1979). **Remarriage.** In *Courtship, Marriage and the Family in Canada,* edited by G.N. Ramu. Toronto: Macmillan of Canada, pp. 153-165. A general overview of remarriage in Canada.

733. Schlesinger, B. (1978). **Remarriage in Canada.** Toronto: Guidance Centre, Faculty of Education, University of Toronto. This booklet discusses remarriage in Canada, and presents detailed findings of a study of 96 couples who married for the second time.

734. Schlesinger, B. (1977). **Husband–Wife Relationships in Reconstituted Families.** *Social Science,* 52, pp. 152-157.

735. Schlesinger, B. (1976). **Children in Reconstituted Families.** *Stepparents' Forum.* Part I, pp. 4-6; Part II, p. 6-7.

736. Schlesinger, B. (1975). **Women and Men in Second Marriages.** In *Marriage, Family and Society,* edited by S.P. Wakil. Toronto: Butterworths.

737. Schlesinger, B. (1974). **The Single Woman in Second Marriages.** *Social Science,* 49, pp. 104-109.

738. Schlesinger, B. (1973). **The Adjustment Process in Remarriage.** *Australian Social Work,* 5, pp. 5-15.

739. Schlesinger, B. (1972). **Remarriage and Children: What's Past is Prologue.** *Australian Social Work,* 4, pp. 17-22.

740. Schlesinger, B. (1971). **Remarriage as Family Reorganization for Divorced Parents.** In *The Canadian Family,* edited by K. Ishwaran. Toronto: Holt, Rinehart and Winston, pp. 377-395.

741. Schlesinger, B. (1970). **Remarriage as Family Reorganization for Divorced Persons — A Canadian Study.** *Journal of Comparative Family Studies,* 1 (1), pp. 101-118.

742. Schlesinger, B. (1968). **Remarriage: An Inventory of Findings.** *The Family Coodinator,* 2, pp. 248-251.

743. Schlesinger, B. and Macrae, A. (1970). **Remarriages in Canada: Statistical Trends.** *Journal of Marriage and the Family,* 32, pp. 300-304.

744. Toth, A.E.S. (1986). **The Remarriage Family: An Alternative for Family Functioning.** *Conciliation Courts Review,* 24, pp. 69-83. A Canadian social worker analyses the remarried family in a conceptual framework.

745. Transition (1986). **Blended Families.** *Transition,* 16. This issue contains two articles related to remarriage in Canada by L. Messinger and A. Thompson-Guppy.

746. Walker, K.N. and Messinger, L. (1979). **Remarriage after Divorce: Dissolution and Reconstruction of Family Boundaries.** *Family Process,* 18, pp. 185-192. The article presents a clear analysis of the tasks faced by family systems in adjusting to divorce and remarriage.

REPRODUCTIVE TECHNOLOGIES AND FAMILY LIFE

747. Ontario Law Reform Commission (1985). **Report on Human Artificial Reproduction and Related Matters.** Toronto: Ministry of the Attorney General.

748. Royal Commission on New Reproductive Technologies (1993). **Proceed with Care: Final Report of the Royal Commission on New Reproductive Technologies.** Ottawa.

SANDWICH GENERATION AND BOOMERANG OFFSPRING

749. Boyd, M. and Norris, D. (1989). **Young Adults Living in Their Parents' Home.** In *Canadian Social Trends.* A Canadian view of young adults who are remaining longer at home.

750. Boyd, M. and Pryor, E.T. (1994). **The Cluttered Nest: The Living Arrangements of Young Canadian Adults.** In *Perspectives on Canada's Population,* edited by F. Trovato and C.F. Grindstaff. Toronto: Oxford University Press, pp. 294-306. Canada's young adults will spend more time in a parental setting.

751. Boyd, M. and Pryor, E.T. (1990). **Young Adults Living in Their Parents' Home.** In *Canadian Social Trends,* edited by C. McKie and K. Thompson. Toronto: Thompson Educational Publishing. A statistical profile of the number of young adult children living at home in Canadian families.

752. Boyd, M. and Pryor, E.T. (1989). **The Cluttered Nest: The Living Arrangements of Young Adult Canadians.** *Canadian Journal of Sociology,* 14 (4), pp. 461-477.

753. Dahlin, K. (1993). **The Sandwich Generation.** *University of Toronto Magazine,* 21 (1), pp. 6-12. A popular article on the Sandwich Generation.

754. Kingsmill, S. and Schlesinger, B. (1998). **The Family Squeeze: Surviving the Sandwich Generation.** Toronto: University of Toronto Press. A guide to Canadians who find themselves in the sandwich generation.

755. MacDonald, S.A. (1988). **An Aging Canada: Sandwich and Caregiver Dilemmas.** *Perspectives,* 12 (1), pp. 15-18. Addressed to nurses, the paper examines caregiving dilemmas. Canadian demographic trends are also included.

756. McDaniel, S.A. (1988). **An Aging Canada: Sandwich and Caregiver Dilemmas.** *Perspectives: Journal of the Gerontological Nursing Association,* 12 (2), pp. 15-18.

757. Mitchell, B. (1998). **Too Close For Comfort? Parental Assessments of "Boomerang Kid" Living Arrangements.** *Canadian Journal of Sociology,* 23 (1), pp. 21-46. A study of 218 Canadian families who experienced the return of an adult child.

758. Mitchell, B. and Gee, E.M. (1996). **Boomerang Kids and Mid–Life Parental Satisfaction.** *Family Relations,* 45, pp. 442-448. A study of 172 parents of boomerang kids in British Columbia. The overall marital satisfaction of the parents is quite high (73% were satisfied).

759. Mitchell, B.A., Wister, A.V. and Burch, T.K. (1989). **The Family Environment and Leaving the Parental Home.** *Journal of Marriage and the Family,* 51, pp. 605-613. This Canadian sample included 14,004 respondents between the ages of 18 and 64. It examines when children leave home in various types of families.

760. Norland, J.A. (1994). **The Sandwich Generation in Canada: Basic Demographic Characteristics.** Ottawa: Statistics Canada, Demography Division. Unpublished paper. This paper documents Canadian family statistics related to the Sandwich Generation.

761. Raphael, D. and Schlesinger, B. (1994). **Women in the Sandwich Generation: Do Adult Children Living at Home Help?** *Journal of Women and Aging,* 6 (12), pp. 21-46. A summary of the first Canadian study of 66 "women in the middle" of the Sandwich Generation.

762. Raphael, D. and Schlesinger, B. (1993). **Caring for Elderly Parents and Children Living at Home: The Sandwich Generation.** *Social Work Research and Abstract,* 29 (1), pp. 3-8. A report on the statistical methodology of a study of 60 "women in the middle" in Metropolitan Toronto.

763. Rosenthal, C.J., Matthews, M. and Matthews, S.H. (1996). **Caught in the Middle: Occupancy in Multiple Roles and Help to Parents in a National Probability Sample of Canadian Adults.** *Journal of Gerontology, Social Sciences,* 51B, S274-83. A sample of 2,703 women and 2,412 men in the age range 35-64 and living in Canada were surveyed by telephone. They were asked how typical the experience was of being "caught in the middle."

764. Schlesinger, B. (1989). **The "Sandwich Generation": Middle–Aged Families Under Stress.** *Canada's Mental Health,* 37, pp. 11-14. A summary of the various layers in the Sandwich Generation. Implications for research are included.

765. Schlesinger, B. and Raphael, D. (1994). **Women in the Sandwich Generation: Do Adult Children Living at Home Help?** *Journal of Women and Aging,* 6, pp. 1-2, 21-46.

766. Schlesinger, B. and Raphael, D. (1993). **The Woman in the Middle: The Sandwich Generation Revisited.** *International Journal of Sociology of the Family,* 23, pp. 77-87. A comprehensive report of the findings of a Canadian study of 66 women who are in the Sandwich Generation.

767. Schlesinger, B. and Raphael, D. (1992). **The Sandwich Generation. The Jewish Woman in the Middle: Stresses and Satisfactions.** *Journal of Psychology and Judaism,* 16 (2), pp. 77-95. Among a study of 66 "women in the middle," there were ten Jewish women. The paper focuses on the responses of this group.

768. Schlesinger, B. and Raphael, D. (1992). **The Sandwich Generation: The Woman in the Middle and Elderly Parents.** *Family Life Educators Association,* pp. 1-3.

769. Usher, C.M. (1995). **Boomerang Kids: When Adult Children Return Home.** Vancouver: B.C. Council for the Family. This pamphlet has a good description of boomerang children, including a contract you can make with the young adult child. (204-2590 Granville Street, Vancouver, BC, V6H 3H1).

770. Veevers, J.E. and Mitchell, B.A. (1998). **Intergenerational Exchanges and Perceptions of Support With "Boomerang–Kid" Family Environments.** *The International Journal of Aging and Human Development,* 46, 2, pp. 91-108. A study of "boomerang" children who return to the home in Vancouver.

SENIORS

771. Abu-Laban, S. (1987). **The Family Life of Older Canadians.** In *Aging in Canada,* edited by Victor W. Marshall. Toronto: Fitzhenry and Whiteside Limited, pp. 123-34.

772. Abu-Laban, S. (1980). **The Family Life of Older Canadians.** In *Aging in Canada: Social Perspectives,* edited by Victor W. Marshall. Toronto: Fitzhenry and Whiteside Limited, pp. 123-34. This article examines the nature of family life in later adulthood by focusing on three specific phases — marriage, widowhood, and remarriage.

773. Abu-Laban, S.M. (1978). **The Family Life of Older Canadians.** *Canadian Home Economics Journal,* pp. 16-25.

774. Baker, M. (1988). **Aging in Canadian Society: A Survey.** Toronto: McGraw-Hill Ryerson. A comprehensive survey of aging in Canada; has an extensive bibliography pp. 124-141.

775. Bayne, R. and Wigdor, B., eds. (1980). **Research Issues in Aging**. Hamilton: Gerontology Research Council of Ontario. Conference papers discuss various aspects of aging in Canada.

776. Béland, F. (1984). **The Family and Adults 65 Years of Age and Over: Co-residency and Availability of Help**. *The Canadian Review of Sociology and Anthropology,* 21, pp. 302-317. A study of francophone elderly persons who were disabled living in a multigenerational household.

777. Burrows, G.D. (1995). **Pension Considerations on Marriage Breakdown at Retirement Age.** *Canadian Family Law Quarterly,* 13, pp. 25-48.

778. Connidis, I.A. (1989). **Family Ties and Aging**. Toronto: Butterworths. A discussion of the wide variety of family ties that are part of older adult life.

779. Connidis, I.A. and McMullin, J. (1994). **Social Support in Older Age: Assessing the Impact of Marital and Parental Status.** *Canadian Journal on Aging,* 13 (4), pp. 510-527.

780. Connidis, I.A. and Rempel, J. (1983). **The Living Arrangements of Older Residents: The Role of Gender, Marital Status, Age and Family Size.** *Canadian Journal on Aging,* 2, pp. 91-105.

781. Desjardins, B. and Dumas, J. (1993). **Population Aging and the Elderly.** Catalogue 91-533E. Ottawa: Statistics Canada.

782. Dulude, L. (1987). **Getting Old: Men in Couples and Women Alone.** In *Women and Men: Interdisciplinary Readings,* edited by G.H. Nemiroff. Toronto: Fitzhenry and Whiteside.

783. Gauthier, P. (1991). **Canada's Seniors.** *Canadian Social Trends,* pp. 16-20.

784. Gee, E.M. (1987). **Historical Change in the Family Life Course of Canadian Men and Women.** In *Aging in Canada,* edited by Victor W. Marshall. Markham: Fitzhenry and Whiteside, pp. 265-287.

785. Gee, E.M. and Kimball, M.K. (1987). **Women and Aging.** Toronto: Butterworths. Highlights the significant relationship between aging and women's issues in Canada.

786. Hagey, J. (1989). **Help Around the House: Support for Older Canadians.** *Canadian Social Trends,* pp. 22-24. What kind of help is given to Canada's elderly in their own homes?

787. Jones, M. (1990). **Time Use of the Elderly.** *Canadian Social Trends,* pp. 28-30. How do Canada's seniors spend their time, including family care?

788. Kryiazis, N. and Stelcner, M. (1986). **A Logit Analysis of Living Arrangements in Canada: A Comparison of the Young and the Aging.** *Journal of Comparative Family Studies,* 17, pp. 389-402. Increasing age, higher education, residence in Western provinces and employment in managerial occupations increases the probability of living alone for both older men and women.

789. Marshall, V. and Rosenthal, C. (1986). **Aging and Later Life.** In *Sociology,* 3rd edition, edited by R. Hagedorn. Toronto: Holt, Rinehart and Winston.

790. Marshall, V.W. (1987). **Aging in Canada: Social Perspectives, 2nd edition.** Section 5, "Family Structure and Social Relationships," Toronto: Fitzhenry and Whiteside. Contains five papers that discuss aging and family life.

791. McDaniel, S.A. (1994). **Emotional Support and Family Contacts of Older Canadians.** In *Canadian Social Trends,* Volume 2, pp. 129-132. Toronto: Thompson. Spouses and adult children are the main sources of emotional support for most Canadian aged 65 and over in 1990.

792. McDaniel, S.A. (1993). **Emotional Support and Family Contacts of Older Canadians.** *Canadian Social Trends,* 28, pp. 30-33.

793. McDaniel, S.A. (1992). **Women and Family in the Later Years: Findings from the 1990 General Social Survey.** *Canadian Woman Studies,* 12 (2), pp. 62-64.

794. McDaniel, S.A. (1986). **Canada's Aging Population.** Toronto: Butterworths. An analysis of the demographic changes related to the elderly population in Canada.

795. National Advisory Council on Aging (1983). **Family Role and the Negotiation of Change for the Aged.** Ottawa. The transitional changes facing older Canadians and the role played by their families is discussed in this paper.

796. Naus, P.J. (1980). **Growing Old.** Toronto: Guidance Centre, Faculty of Education, University of Toronto. A booklet that discusses aging in Canada.

797. Nett, E.M. (1984). **The Family and Aging.** In *The Family,* edited by M. Baker. Toronto: McGraw-Hill Ryerson.

798. Nett, E.M. (1980). **The Family.** In *Sociology,* edited by R. Hagedorn. Toronto: Holt, Rinehart and Winston, pp. 353-386. An overview of the Canadian family.

799. Northcott, H.C. (1988). **Changing Residence: The Geographic Mobility of Elderly Canadians.** Toronto: Butterworths. A discussion of the patterns of geographic mobility of elderly Canadians.

800. Novak, M. (1988). **Aging and Society: A Canadian Perspective.** Toronto: Nelson Canada. An extensive overview of aging in Canada including family life and social supports.

801. Posner, J. (1980). **Old and Female: The Double Whammy.** In *Aging in Canada: Social Perspectives,* edited by V. Marshall. Toronto: Fitzhenry and Whiteside, pp. 80-87. This article examines the meaning of aging in our society particularly as it affects women, using an interesting perspective — the perspective of the body.

802. Rosenthal, C. (1987). **Aging and Intergenerational Relations in Canada.** In *Aging in Canada,* 2nd edition, edited by Victor Marshall, pp. 311-335. Toronto: Fitzhenry and Whiteside. Research has destroyed the myth that elder persons are isolated from and abandoned by their families.

803. Schwenger, C.W. and Gross, J. (1980). **Institutional Care and Institutionalization of the Elderly in Canada.** In *Aging in Canada: Social Perspectives,* edited by Victor W. Marshall. Toronto: Fitzhenry and Whiteside, pp. 248-256. Institutional care and institutionalization of the aged in Canada is examined in this article using demographic variables and classifications of the type of institutional care (1976).

804. Stone, L.L. and Fletcher, S. (1980). **A Profile of Canada's Older Population.** Montreal: The Institute for Research on Public Policy.

805. Stone, L.O. and Fletcher, S. (1986). **The Seniors Boom.** Ottawa: Minister of Supply and Services. A chartbook that highlights the older population in Canada.

806. Strain, L. and Payne, B.J. (1992). **Social Networks and Patterns of Social Interaction Among Ever–Single and Separated/Divorced Elderly Canadians.** *Canadian Journal on Aging,* 11 (1), pp. 31-53.

807. Termote, M. (1990). **The Aged and the Family Environment.** *Canadian Studies in Population,* 17, pp. 45-51.

808. Transition (1988). **Some Good News About Aging.** *Transition*, 18, Special Issue. Articles discuss aging in Canada, and family life.

SEXUAL ISSUES IN FAMILY LIFE

809. Badgley, A.W. (1984). **Report of the Federal Committee on Sexual Offences Against Children and Youths.** Ottawa: Federal Departments of Justice, and Health and Welfare.

810. Bibby, R.W. (1983). **The Moral Mosaic: Sexuality in the Canadian 1980s.** *Social Indicators Research,* 13, pp. 171-184.

811. Byers, E., Heinlein, S. and Heinlein, L. (1989). **Predicting Initiations and Refusal of Sexual Activities in Married and Cohabiting Heterosexual Couples.** *The Journal of Sex Research,* 26, pp. 210-231.

812. Herold, E.S. (1984). **Sexual Behaviour of Canadian Young People.** Markham: Fitzhenry and Whiteside.

813. Hobart, C.W. (1972). **Sexual Permissiveness in Young English and French Canadians.** *Journal of Marriage and the Family,* 34, pp. 292-303.

814. Orton, M.J. and Rosenblatt, E. (1986). **Adolescent Pregnancy in Ontario: Progress in Prevention.** Toronto: Planned Parenthood of Ontario. A report related to an examination of adolescent pregnancy and suggestions for preventive programs.

815. Orton, M.J. and Rosenblatt, E. (1981). **Adolescent Birth Planning Needs: Ontario in the Eighties.** Toronto: Planned Parenthood of Ontario. An examination of adolescent pregnancies over the years 1975–78.

816. Pool, J.S. and Pool, D.I. (1978). **Contraception and Health Care Among Young Canadian Women.** Ottawa: Carleton University Press.

817. Schlesinger, B. (1977). **Sexual Behaviour in Canada: Patterns and Problems.** Toronto: University of Toronto Press.

818. Schlesinger, B., ed. (1974). **Family Planning in Canada: A Source Book.** Toronto: University of Toronto Press. Thirty-four articles discuss various aspects related to family planning in Canada.

SINGLEHOOD

819. Austrom, D. (1985). **Psychological Issues of Single Life in Canada: An Exploratory Study.** *International Journal of Women's Studies,* 8 (1), pp. 12-23. A summary of the author's study on single persons in Canada.

820. Austrom, D.R. (1984). **The Consequences of Being Single.** New York: Peter Lang. A study of single persons in Canada.

821. Peters, J. (1983). **The Single Female.** In *Marriage and Divorce in Canada,* edited by K. Ishwaran, pp. 107-125. Toronto: Methuen.

822. Todres, R. (1979). **Singlehood.** In *Families: Canada,* edited by B. Schlesinger. Toronto: McGraw-Hill Ryerson, pp. 136-140. A study of 86 single women and 29 single men completed in Metropolitan Toronto.

SOCIAL POLICY AND THE FAMILY

823. Alberta (1992). **Family Policy Grid.** Edmonton: Premier's Council in Support of Alberta's Families. This report develops a family grid to help and support public policies.

824. Baker, M. (1998). **Women, Family Policies and the Moral Right.** *Canadian Review of Social Policy,* 40 (40), pp. 47-64. Social programs to help Canadian women and families combine paid work and family life have not kept pace with the need.

825. Baker, M. (1995). **Canadian Family Policies: Cross–National Comparisons.** Toronto: University of Toronto Press. Compares family policies in Canada, Australia, France, Germany and the United States.

826. Bala, N. (1991). **Child and Family Policies for the 1990s.** In *Children, Families and Public Policy in the 90s,* edited by L. C. Johnson and D. Barnhorst. Toronto: Thompson Educational Publishing.

827. Béland, F. (1986). **Living Arrangement Preferences among the Quebec Elderly: Findings and Policy Implications.** *Canadian Social Policy,* 12 (1), pp. 175-189.

828. Chappell, N. (1980). **Social Policy and the Elderly.** In *Aging in Canada,* edited by V.W. Marshall, pp. 35-42. Toronto: Fitzhenry and Whiteside.

829. Evans, P. (1988). **Work Incentives and the Single Mother: Dilemmas of Reform.** *Canadian Public Policy,* 14, pp. 125-136. Wage supplements cannot meet the objective of encouraging social assistance recipients to enter full-time work.

830. Gee, E.M. and McDaniel, S.A. (1992). **Social Policy for an Aging Canada.** *Journal of Canadian Studies,* 27 (3), pp. 139-152.

831. Guest, D. (1980). **The Emergence of Social Security in Canada.** Vancouver: University of British Columbia Press.

832. Harlton, S., Keating, N. and Fast, J. (1998). **Defining Eldercare for Policy and Practice: Perspectives Matter.** *Family Relations,* 47, pp. 281-288. A discussion of eldercare in Canada.

833. Health and Welfare Canada (1988). **Income Security Programs.** Ottawa. Booklets are available that describe the Canada Pension Plan, Old Age Security, Survivor Benefits, Guaranteed Income and other programs for Canada's elderly. Updated regularly.

834. Income Security Programs, Canada (1987). **Booklets.** Ottawa: Heath and Welfare Canada. Booklets are available to explain Family Allowances, Canada Pension Plan, Old Age Security Pension, and Survivor Benefits. These federal programs are all geared to support family life. Updated regularly.

835. Johnson, L.C. and Barnhorst, D., eds. (1991). **Children, Families and Public Policy in the 90s.** Toronto: Thompson Educational Publishing.

836. Kitchen, B. (1997). **The New Child Benefit: Much Ado About Nothing.** *Canadian Review of Social Policy*, 39, Spring, pp. 65-73.

837. Kitchen, B. (1984). **The Family and Social Policy.** In *The Family: Changing Trends in Canada,* edited by M. Baker. Toronto: Macmillan, pp. 178-187. An examination of family policies in Canada.

838. Laurin, C.A. (1984). **A Working Paper on Family Policy.** Quebec: Ministry of Social Affairs. The "green paper" discusses what a family policy could entail and encompass in Quebec.

839. Le Bourdais, C. and Marcil-Gratton, N. (1994). **Quebec's Pro–Active Approach to Family Policy: Thinking and Acting Family.** In *Canada's Changing Families: Challenges to Public Policy,* edited by M. Baker. Ottawa: Vanier Institute of the Family.

840. Madison, B. (1964). **Canadian Family Allowances and their Major Social Implications.** *Journal of Marriage and the Family,* 26 (2), pp. 134-142.

841. McDaniel, S.A. (1990). **Towards Family Policy with Women in Mind.** *Feminist Perspectives.* Ottawa: Canadian Research Institute for the Advancement of Women.

842. McDaniel, S.A. (1987). **Demographic Aging as A Guiding Paradigm in Canada's Welfare State.** *Canadian Public Policy,* 13, pp. 330-336. The central argument of this paper is that demographic aging has emerged as an important guiding paradigm in Canadian public policy discussion and research.

843. Rochon, M. (1986). **Collective Support Demanded for Quebec Families.** Quebec: Secretariat for Family Policies. To discuss the implications of the "green paper." The report comes in Part 1 and Part 2.

844. Ryant, J.C. (1980). **Social Policy and the Canadian Family.** In *Perspectives on Family Therapy,* edited by D.S. Freeman. Vancouver: Butterworths. A description and analysis of family-related social policy in Canada.

845. Social Planning Council of Metropolitan Toronto (1983). **The Family in our Community: Background for Social Policy.** Toronto: SPCM. The role of the family in Canadian society.

846. Strong-Boag, V. (1979). **Wages for Housework: Mothers' Allowances and the Beginnings of Social Security in Canada.** *Journal of Canadian Studies,* 14, pp. 24-34.

847. Yelaja, S.A., ed. (1987). **Canadian Social Policy, revised edition.** Waterloo: Wilfrid Laurier University Press. Three chapters deal with social policy concerning women, child welfare policy, and social policy and the elderly.

848. Younge, E. (1945). **Canada's Family Allowance Act 1944.** *American Sociological Review,* 10, pp. 429-430.

STRENGTHS OF FAMILIES

849. Alberta (1993). **Perspectives on Family Well-Being.** Edmonton: Premier's Council in Support of Alberta's Families. This report focusses on the positive aspects of family life in Alberta.

850. Schlesinger, B. (1998). **Strengths in Families: Accentuating the Positive.** Ottawa: Vanier Institute of the Family. *Contemporary Family Trends* (a position paper). A review of the Canadian and American literature related to strengths in families.

851. Schlesinger, B. (1983). **Lasting and Functioning Marriages in the 1980s.** *Canadian Journal of Community Mental Health,* 2, pp. 45-56.

852. Schlesinger, B. (1982). **Lasting Marriages in the 1980s.** *Conciliation Courts Review,* 20, pp. 43-49. The authors reviews the material available on lasting marriages. He also includes the results of a study of 129 couples that he conducted concerning lasting marriages.

853. Schlesinger, B. and Schlesinger, R. (1987). **Lasting Marriages and Families: Accentuating the Positive.** *Pastoral Sciences,* 6, pp. 25-38. A review of the literature on lasting marriages and families.

WOMEN AND FAMILY LIFE: OVERVIEW

854. Bird, F., Chair (1970). **Report of the Royal Commission on the Status of Women in Canada.** Ottawa: Information Canada.

855. Canadian Woman Studies (1998). **Looking Back, Looking Forward: Mothers, Daughters, and Feminism.** *Canadian Woman Studies,* 18, 2/3, Summer/Fall, Special Double Issue.

856. Chekki, D.A. (1976). **The Changing Roles of Women in Canada.** *Sociologia Internationalis,* 14, pp. 201-219.

857. Cohen, L. (1984). **Small Expectations: Society's Betrayal of Older Women.** Toronto: McClelland and Stewart. Explores society's treatment of women as they age in Canada.

858. Doerr, A. and Carrier, M., eds. (1981). **Women and the Constitution.** Ottawa: The Canadian Advisory Council on the Status of Women. Fourteen papers discuss women and the Constitution. The topics include divorce, marriage breakdown, and women and poverty.

859. Dulude, L. (1978). **Women and Aging.** Ottawa: The Canadian Advisory Council on the Status of Women. The author presents a report or general overview of the status of aging and elderly women in Canada.

860. Dumont, M., et al. (1987). **Quebec Women: A History.** Toronto: Women's Press.

861. Eichler, M. (1983). **Women, Families and the State.** In *Perspectives on Women in the 1980s,* edited by Joan Turner and Lois Emery. Winnipeg: University of Manitoba Press.

862. Eichler, M. (1973). **Women as Personal Dependents.** In *Women in Canada,* edited by Marylee Stephenson. Toronto: New Press, pp. 36-55.

863. Landsberg, M. (1983). **Women and Children First.** Toronto: Penguin. An examination of Canadian women at work and at home.

864. McDaniel, S.A. (1992). **The Changing Canadian Family: Women's Roles and the Impact of Feminism.** In *Changing Patterns: Women in Canada,* edited by S. Burt, et al. Toronto: McClelland and Stewart.

865. McDaniel, S.A. (1988). **The Changing Canadian Family: Women's Roles and the Impact of Feminism.** In *Changing Patterns: Women in Canada,* edited by S. Burt, L. Code and L. Dorney. Toronto: McClelland and Stewart, pp. 103-128. The most salient family changes in Canada are covered in this chapter. The decrease

in family size, increased participation of married women in the labour force, and marital dissolution are reviewed.

866. Ontario Advisory Council on Women's Issues (1988). **Motherhood in a Changing Society.** Toronto. The proceedings of a conference held in June 1988 on the topic of motherhood.

867. Smith, D.E. (1985). **Women, Class and Family.** In *Women, Class, Family and the State,* edited by V. Burstyn and D.E. Smith. Toronto: Garamond.

868. Smith, D.E. (1981). **Women's Inequality and the Family.** In *Inequality: Essays on the Political Economy of Social Welfare,* edited by A. Moscovitch and G. Drover. Toronto: University of Toronto Press.

869. Smith, D.E. (1973). **Women, the Family and Corporate Capitalism.** In *Women in Canada,* edited by Marylee Stephenson. Toronto: New Press, pp. 2-35.

870. Stephenson, M., ed. (1977). **Women in Canada.** Toronto: General Publishing. Fourteen selections discuss varied issues related to Canadian women including motherhood. A good bibliography on Canadian women, 1950–1975, is included.

WOMEN AND FAMILY LIFE: WORK AND FAMILY

871. Armstrong, P. and Armstrong, H. (1988). **The Conflicting Demands of "Work" and "Home."** In *Family Matters: Sociology and Contemporary Families,* edited by K.L. Anderson, et al. Toronto: Nelson.

872. Armstrong, P. and Armstrong, H. (1984). **The Double Ghetto, Canadian Women and their Segregated Work, 2nd edition.** Toronto McClelland and Stewart.

873. Canadian Women Studies (1998). **Women and Work: The Second Shift.** *Canadian Women Studies,* 18 (1), Special Issue. The articles examine women and work and some of the complexity of paid and unpaid work.

874. Conference Board of Canada (1994). **The Work and Family Challenge: Issues and Options.** Ottawa. A discussion of work and family issues in the Canadian context.

875. Duffy, A. and Pupo, N. (1992). **Part–Time Paradox: Connecting Gender, Work and Family.** Toronto: McClelland and Stewart.

876. Evans, P. and Pupo, N. (1993). **Parental Leave: Assessing Women's Interests.** *Canadian Journal of Women and the Law,* 6, pp. 402-418.

877. Labour Canada, Women's Bureau (1988). **Leave for Employees with Family Responsibilities.** Ottawa: Labour Canada. This study examines the question of leave for workers with family responsibilities, primarily women.

878. Lero, D.S. and Johnson, K.L. (1994). **110 Canadian Statistics on Work and Family.** Ottawa: The Canadian Advisory Council on the Status of Women. A compendium of research findings drawn from the most recent national studies and data sources in Canada.

879. Marshall, K. (1994). **Balancing Work and Family Responsibilities.** *Perspectives on Labour and Income*, 6 (1), pp. 26-30.

880. Marshall, K. (1993). **Employed Parents and the Division of Housework.** *Perspectives on Labour and Income*, Catalogue 75-001E. Statistics Canada.

881. Maureen, M. (1989). **Dual Earner Families: The New Norm.** *Canadian Social Trends*, pp. 24-26.

882. Roberts, W.L. (1989). **Two Career Families: Demographic Variables, Parenting and Competence in Young Children.** *Canadian Journal of Behavioural Science,* 19, pp. 347-356.

883. Schlesinger, B. and Schlesinger, R. (1983). **Juggling Careers: A View From Both Sides.** *Canadian Home Economics Journal,* 33, pp. 117-119. This article discusses dual working couples in Canada.

884. Smith, D.E. (1990). **Women's Work as Mothers: A New Look at the Relation of Class, Family and School Achievement.** In *Feminism and Education: A Canadian Perspective,* edited by F. Forman. Toronto: Centre for Women's Studies in Education, Ontario Institute for Studies in Education.

885. Stone, L. (1994). **Dimensions of Job–Family Tension.** Ottawa: Statistics Canada.

WOMEN: SOCIETAL ISSUES

886. Appleby, B.M. (1999). **Responsible Parenthood: Decriminalizing Contraception in Canada.** Toronto: University of Toronto Press.

887. Bakan, A. and Stasiulis, D. (1997). **Not One of the Family: Foreign Domestic Workers in Canada.** Toronto: University of Toronto Press, Toronto.

888. Begin, M. (1982). **Wife–Battering: A National Concern.** Ottawa: Health and Welfare Canada.

889. Bess, I. (1999). **Widows Living Alone.** *Canadian Social Trends,* 53, pp. 2-5.

890. Boyd, M. (1984). **Canadian Attitudes Towards Women: Thirty Years of Change.** Ottawa: Labour Canada. An analysis of Canadian Gallup polls dating back to 1953 and related to Canadian women.

891. Burstyn, V. and Smith, D. (1985). **Women, Class, Family and the State.** Toronto: Garamond Press.

892. Burt, S., Code, L. and Dorney, L. (1988). **Changing Patterns: Women in Canada.** Toronto: McClelland and Stewart. An account of past and present changes in Canadian women's lives.

893. Che-Alford, J. and Hamm, B. (1999). **Under One Roof: Three Generations Living Together.** *Canadian Social Trends,* 53, pp. 6-9.

894. Cook, R. and Mitchinson, W. (1976). **Their Proper Sphere: Woman's Place in Canadian Society.** Toronto: Oxford University Press.

895. Killoran, M.M. (1984). **The Management of Tension: A Case Study of Chatelaine Magazine 1939–1980.** *Journal of Comparative Family Studies,* 15, pp. 407-426. A content analysis of articles in Chatelaine related to women.

896. Labour Canada, Women's Bureau (1990). **Women in the Labour Force. 1990–91 Edition.** Ottawa: Minister of Supply and Services.

897. Labour Canada (1986). **Women in the Labour Force 1985–1986 Edition.** Ottawa: Minister of Supply and Services.

898. MacLellan, M.E. (1971). **History of Women's Rights in Canada.** *Cultural Tradition and Political History of Women in Canada,* No. 8. Studies of the Royal Commission on the Status of Women in Canada. Ottawa: Information Canada.

899. Nelson, E.D. and Robinson, B.W. (1998). **Gender in Canada.** Toronto: Prentice-Hall Canada.

900. Petrie, A. (1999). **Gone to an Aunt's: Remembering Canada's Homes for Unwed Mothers.** Toronto: McClelland and Stewart.

901. Prentice, A., Bourne, P., Cuthbert-Brandt, G., Light, B., Mitchinson, W., and Black, N. (1988). **Canadian Women: A History.** Toronto: Holt, Rinehart and Winston. The lives of Canadian women from the days of European settlement to the present.

902. Pupo, N. (1988). **Preserving Patriarchy: Women, the Family and the State.** In *Life-Span Development and Behavior,* 4, edited by P.B. Baltes and O.G. Brim. New York: Academic Press.

903. Royal Commission on the Status of Women (1970). **Report.** Ottawa: Information Canada. The Commission examined the steps to be taken by the federal government to ensure Canadian women equal opportunities. The chairperson was Mrs. J. Bird.

904. Schlesinger, R. (1987). **Jewish Women: Beyond the Stereotype.** In *Jewish Family Issues: A Resource Guide,* edited by B. Schlesinger. New York: Garland Press, pp. 34-54. A review of the place of Jewish women throughout history.

RELATED TOPICS: FAMILY ISSUES

905. Council for Families (1999). **Family Connection.** *Special Issue: Stepfamilies: Building for Success.* Vancouver: B.C. Council for Families, 6 (2). This journal is published four times per year on different family topics. (To order: #204-2590 Granville St., Vancouver, BC, V6H 3H1).

906. Daly, K.J. (1996). **Families and Time: Keeping Pace in a Hurried Culture.** Thousand Oaks: Sage Publications. What is family time and what value do we place on it? How do families control time?

907. Duffy, A. and Momirov, J. (1997). **Family Violence: A Canadian Introduction.** Toronto: James Lorimer & Co.

908. Forbes, W.F., Jackson, J.A. and Kraus, A.S. (1987). **Institutionalization of the Elderly in Canada.** Toronto: Butterworths. An examination of the existing research, policies, programs and practices related to the health care system for the elderly.

909. Glossop, R. (1994). Robert Glossop on the Canadian Family. *Canadian Social Trends,* 30, pp. 2-10. A general overview on Canadian families in 1994.

910. Juby, H. And LeBourdais, C. (1998). **The Changing Context of Fatherhood in Canada: A Life Course Analysis.** *Population Studies,* 55 (2) July, pp. 163-176.

911. McDaniel, S.A. and Mitchinson, W. (1988). **Family Fictions in Canadian Literature.** Waterloo: University of Waterloo Press.

912. McDonald, P.L., Hornick, J.P., Robertson, G.B. and Wallace, J.E. (1991). **Elder Abuse and Neglect in Canada.** Toronto: Butterworths.

913. Montgomery, B.G., Myers, H.D. and Kreller, D.G. (1986). **Marriage and Family Life: A Multifaith Heritage.** Victoria: B.C. Council for the Family. A discussion of marriage and family life and the religious influences on the Canadian family mosaic.

914. Morrison, J., ed. (1965). **The Canadian Conference on the Family.** Ottawa: Vanier Institute of the Family. A summary of the first conference on the family in Ottawa, June 7-19, 1964.

915. Moscovitch, A. (1999). **Electronic Media and the Family.** Ottawa: Vanier Institute of the Family. *Contemporary Family Trends (*a position paper). This paper examines media messages and media experiences in the context of the family.

916. Podnieks, E., Pillemer, K., Nicholson, J., Shillington, J. and Frizzell, A. (1989). **National Survey on Abuse of the Elderly in Canada: Preliminary Findings.** Toronto: Office of Research and Innovation, Ryerson Polytechnical Institute.

917. Schlesinger, B., ed. (1970). **The Multi–Problem Family: A Review and Annotated Bibliography, 3rd edition.** Toronto: University of Toronto Press. A discussion of multi-problem families in Canada and the United States.

918. Schlesinger, B. (1965). **The Canadian Conference on the Family.** *Journal of Marriage and the Family,* 27, pp. 6-8.

919. Shorter, E. (1975). **The Making of the Modern Family.** New York: Basic Books. A comprehensive history of the modern family in Western culture.

920. Timpson, J. (1995). **Four Decades of Literature on Native Canadian Child Welfare: Changing Themes.** *Child Welfare,* 74, pp. 525-546.

921. Transition (1999). **Family Life: Past, Present, Future.** *Transition,* 29 (4), Special Issue. Three articles focus on lessons from history, the family at mid-century and look to the future for Canada's families.

922. Vanier Institute of the Family (1999). **Transition.** *Special Issues: Lone Parents and their Families,* 29 (1); *Families and the Almighty Dollar,* 29 (2); *Young Canadians,* 29 (3). These are some editions of the journal *Transition,* published by the Vanier Institute of the Family. Each contains articles related to the topic.

923. Vanier Institute of the Family (1996). **Canada's Families — They Count.** Ottawa: Vanier Institute of the Family. A notebook that contains demographic trends related to families in Canada up to 1994.

924. Watt, D. and White, J.M. (1999). **Computers and Family Life: A Family Development Perspective.** *Journal of Comparative Family Studies,* 130 (1), pp.

1-16. This paper reviews the issues and research findings related to the effects of computer use on the family.

925. White, J.M. (1999). **Work–Family Stage and Satisfaction with Work Family Balance.** *Journal of Comparative Family Studies,* 30 (2), pp. 163-176. Canadian findings related to work and the family stages.

RELATED TOPICS: FAMILY RESEARCH

926. Data Base. **Exploring Canada on the Digital Frontier.** *Early Canadiana Online.* Particular strengths of the database include English Canadian literature (with accounts of travel and discovery), women's history, native studies, history of French Canada, 19th Century French Canadian Literature. Twenty-four hour/day access to 3,200 complete books and pamphlets online. Search in English or French, www.canadiana.org

927. Douthitt, R. (1984). **Canadian Family Time Use Data: Current Status and Future Prospects.** *Canadian Home Economics Journal,* 34, pp. 109-113.

928. Social Sciences and Humanities Research Council (1994). **Canadian Research on Family Issues.** Ottawa: SSHRC. This booklet lists close to 475 projects funded by the SSHRC during the 1978–1993 period.

929. Spencer, J. (1967). **An Inventory of Family Research and Studies in Canada (1963–1967).** Ottawa: Vanier Institute of the Family. An annotated list of available Canadian family studies.

930. Wargon, S.T. (1972). **Using Census Data for Research on the Family in Canada.** *Journal of Comparative Family Studies,* 3 (1), pp. 162-167.

RELATED TOPICS: FAMILY SURVEYS

931. Campaign 2000 (1999). **Report Card on Child Poverty in Canada: 1989–1999.** Toronto: Family Service Association. This booklet illustrates the demographic trends related to Canada's poor children.

932. Canada, Human Resources Department (1999). **Applied Research Bulletin, Special Edition on Child Development.** Ottawa: Human Resources Development, Fall. Fourteen summaries of Canadian studies related to various aspects of child development.

933. Canadian Council on Social Development (1996). **The Progress of Canada's Children, 1996.** Ottawa: Canadian Council on Social Development. Measures the

indicators of the well-being of Canada's children from year to year. One fifth of Canada's children are poor.

934. Keating, N., Fast, J., Frederick, J., Cranswick, K. and Perrier, C. (1999). **Eldercare in Canada: Context, Content and Consequences.** Ottawa: Statistics Canada, Catalogue #89-570-XPE (November). The result of the 1996 General Social Survey (GSS) on informal eldercare in Canada. Contains a good bibliography (pp. 107-116).

935. Lero, D.S., Brockman, L.M., Pence, A.R., Goelman, H. and Johnson, K.L. (1992). **Canadian National Child Care Study.** Ottawa: Statistics Canada. A comprehensive national survey of Canadian families with at least one child under the age of 18. The study also includes a review and history of child care in each province and territory. There are seven reports available related to the study (see #69, #72, #74).

936. Lindsay, C. and Almey, A. (1999). **A Portrait of Seniors in Canada, 3rd edition.** Ottawa: Statistics Canada, Catalogue #89-519-XPE. A comprehensive set of indicators describing the demographic profile of seniors as well as their family and living arrangements.

937. National Council of Welfare (1999). **Poverty Profile 1997.** Ottawa: National Council of Welfare. An Annual Report that summarizes the poverty rates in Canada. In 1997, a total of 5.1 million Canadians were poor. This includes 17.2 percent of children, women and men.

938. Statistics Canada (1996). **Canadian Families: Diversity and Change.** Ottawa: General Social Survey, Statistics Canada, Catalogue #12F-0061-XPE. The General Social Survey (GSS) conducted since 1985 gathers data on social trends and policy issues. It covers all persons aged 15 and over residing in private households in the ten provinces.

939. Statistics Canada, Human Resources Development (1996). **Growing Up in Canada.** Ottawa: Statistics Canada, Catalogue #89-550-MPE-No. 1. This document is part of the "National Longitudinal Survey of Children and Youth." Ten papers discuss children in the 1990s, one-parent families, step-families, parenting and adolescence.

RELATED TOPICS: POPULATION STUDIES

940. Balakrishnan, T.R., Lapierre-Adamczyk, E. and Krotki, K.K. (1993). **Family and Childbearing in Canada: A Demographic Analysis.** Toronto: University of Toronto Press. A summary of findings of the National Fertility study completed in 1984.

941. Beaujot, R. (1991). **Population Change in Canada: The Challenges of Policy Adaptation.** Toronto: McClelland and Stewart. A survey of the changing populations in Canada. Policies are considered that will shape the Canadian population and the Canadian future.

RELATED TOPICS: SOURCE BOOKS

942. Marsh, James H. (2000). **The Canadian Encyclopedia.** Toronto: McClelland & Stewart. Consult entries related to varied aspects of Canadian family life.

943. National Council of Welfare (1999). **A Pension Primer.** Ottawa: National Council of Welfare. A guide to Canadians who have no special expertise in pensions. The retirement income system is explained.

ABOUT THE AUTHOR

Benjamin Schlesinger received his Bachelor of Arts (Sociology) from Sir George Williams University, Montreal in 1951, his Master of Social Work in 1953 from the University of Toronto and his Ph.D. in Family Relations from Cornell University in 1961. Since 1960 he has been on staff of the Faculty of Social Work, University of Toronto, becoming a full Professor in 1970. He has been a visiting professor at Universities all over the world and is the author or editor of 23 books. He has co-authored three books with his wife, Rachel, and has written or contributed internationally to more than 250 papers for academic journals. In May 1993 he became the first Canadian professor of social work to be elected a Fellow of the Royal Society of Canada. In 1994, he became a Professor Emeritus. His latest book, *The Family Squeeze: Surviving the Sandwich Generation* (with Suzanne Kingsmill) was published by the University of Toronto Press in 1999.

AUTHOR INDEX (768 AUTHORS)

A

Abell, C.: *385*
Abell, H.C.: *386, 387, 388*
Abella, R.S.: *557*
Abernathy, T.: *558*
Abosh, B.: *619*
Abrahamson, U.: *463*
Abu-Laban, S.: *236, 771, 772*
Abu-Laban, S.M.: *773*
Ackerman, R.J.: *20, 620*
Adams, M.: *35*
Adams, O.: *121, 604*
Adams, O.B.: *122, 123*
Agbayewa, M.W.: *400*
Alberta Committee on Children and Youth: *40*
Alberta: *823, 849*
Allan, C.: *138*
Allingham, J.D.: *411*
Almey, A.: *936*
Ambert, A.M.: *41, 42, 59, 178, 179, 180, 197, 198, 199, 200, 201, 202, 203, 676, 711*
Ames, M.M.: *237*
Anderson, A.: *238*
Anderson, K.L.: *104, 105*
Angus Reid Group: *36*
Anthony, S.: *391*
Appleby, B.M.: *886*
Arat-Koc, S.: *525*
Arcus, M.: *558*
Armstrong, H.: *871, 872*
Armstrong, P.: *222, 871, 872*
Arnold, R.: *677*
Arnup, K.: *437, 438, 439, 440*
Aronson, J.: *312, 313*
Ashworth, M.: *239*
Aubé, N.: *585*
Austin, C.: *672*
Austrom, D.: *819*
Austrom, D.R.: *820*

B

Backhouse, C.B.: *464, 465*
Badgley, A.W.: *809*
Bagnell, K.: *466*
Baines, C.: *377*
Bakan, A.: *887*
Baker, M.: *106, 107, 204, 205, 678, 774, 824, 825*
Bala, N.: *43, 559, 560, 826*
Balakrishnan, T.R.: *75, 81, 103, 411, 940*
Barclay, H.B.: *240*
Barnes, G.E.: *44*
Barnhorst, D.: *835*
Barr, L.: *124*
Bartoletti, L.: *586*
Bartoletti, M.: *586*
Basavarajappa, K.G.: *125*
Bayne, R.: *775*
Beaujot, R.: *126, 127, 128, 129, 941*
Beaujot, R.P.: *130*
Begin, M.: *888*
Béland, F.: *776, 827*
Bélanger, A.: *145*
Belle, M.: *666*
Belliveau, J.A.: *89, 153*
Benjamin, M.: *181, 187, 188, 194*
Bess, I.: *889*
Bhargava, G.: *241*
Bibby, R.G.: *38*
Bibby, R.W.: *45, 810*
Billson, G.: *467*
Bird, F.: *854*
Bisset-Johnson, A.: *561*
Black, N.: *901*
Blain, J.M.M.: *320*
Boissevain, J.: *242, 243, 244*
Boivin, S.P.: *562*
Bond, J.B.: *245*
Borowski, H.: *667*
Bosher, J.F.: *468*
Bouchard, G.: *469*
Bourne, P.: *901*
Bourque, D.M.: *182*
Bouvier, L.F.: *412*
Boyd, M.: *131, 132, 679, 749, 750, 751, 752, 890*
Bracher, M.D.: *346*

Bradbury, B.: *223, 470, 471, 472, 473*
Brayfield, A.A.: *517*
Breton, R.: *46*
Bridge, K.: *224*
Briggs, J.L.: *246*
Brockman, L.M.: *72, 644, 935*
Brockman, L: *69*
Brown, D.: *712, 720*
Brown, J.S.H.: *474*
Brownstone, M.: *389*
Buckley, K.A.H.: *515*
Bullen, M.: *328*
Burch, T.K.: *58, 90, 133, 134, 713, 759*
Burke, M.A.: *47, 631*
Burrows, G.D.: *777*
Burstyn, V.: *891*
Burt, S.: *892*
Burtch, B.E.: *563*
Butlin, G.: *138*
Byers, E.: *811*

C

Caitlin, G.: *135*
Campaign 2000: *931*
Campbell, D.F.: *587*
Canada, Human Resources Department: *932*
Canadian Advisory Council on the Status of Women: *63, 390*
Canadian Child Welfare Association: *703*
Canadian Council on Social Development: *933*
Canadian Historical Association: *247*
Canadian Journal of Community Mental Health: *621*
Canadian Woman Studies: *855*
Canadian Women Studies: *873*
Caputo, T.C.: *564*
Carisse, C.: *530, 531*
Carnet: *314*
Carrier, M.: *858*
Carrier, P.J.: *518*
Chalam-Zukewich, N.: *136*
Chan, K.G.: *308*
Chapman, T.: *475*
Chappell, N.: *257, 828*
Chappell, N.L.: *315*
Charles, E.: *137, 391*
Che-Alford, J.: *138, 893*

Cheal, D.: *588*
Cheal, D.J.: *225*
Chekki, D.A.: *856*
Chimbos, P.D.: *248, 532*
Christensen, C.: *249*
Christiansen, J.M.: *250*
Clarke, K.L.: *559*
Cliche, A.M.: *476*
Clubb, A.N.: *714*
Coalition for Lesbian and Gay Rights in Ontario: *441*
Code, L.: *892*
Cohen, J.S.: *1*
Cohen, L.: *857*
Cohn, W.: *589*
Collins, A.: *619*
Comacchio, C.: *477*
Conference Board of Canada: *874*
Connidis, I.: *546, 779*
Connidis, I.A.: *778, 780*
Conway, J.F.: *323*
Cook, D.: *680*
Cook, R.: *894*
Cooke, K.: *64*
Corbett, G.H.: *478*
Corbett, R.: *528*
Cork, R.M.: *622*
Council for Families: *905*
Cowan, B.: *226*
Cranswick, K.: *934*
Cregheur, A.: *48*
Crompton, S.: *47*
Cruikshank, J.: *251*
Crysdale, S.: *324, 325*
Curtis, J.: *117*
Curtis, J.E.: *541*
Cuthbert-Brandt, G.: *901*

D

Dahlin, K.: *753*
Daly, K.: *2, 17*
Daly, K.J.: *3, 906*
Damas, D.: *252*
Danaher, A.: *702*
Danziger, K.: *253, 254*

Darroch, G.: *479*
Data Base: *926*
Davids, L.: *326, 637, 715*
Davies, C.: *565*
Davies, L.: *518, 668*
Davis, J.C.: *285*
Davitt, P.: *480*
Day, D.: *442, 561*
de Ruyter, B.: *590*
den Boggende, B.: *591*
Denholm, C.: *65*
Dennis, W.: *183*
Department of Justice, Canada: *191, 566, 567*
Desjardins, B.: *781*
Devereaux, M.S.: *48, 139, 140*
Devlin, A.: *192*
Dineen, J.: *67*
Disman, M.: *255*
Doerr, A.: *858*
Dominic, K.: *409*
Dominic, K.T.: *401*
Dominion Bureau of Statistics: *141*
Donnelly, F.K.: *481*
Dooley, M.D.: *704*
Dorney, L.: *892*
Douthitt, R.: *927*
Douthitt, R.A.: *49*
Drakich, J.: *184*
Draper, P.J.: *256*
Driedger, L.: *238, 257, 533*
Duchesne, D.: *519*
Duff, A.: *459*
Duffy, A.: *875, 907*
Dulude, L.: *227, 782, 859*
Dumas, J.: *142, 143, 144, 145, 146, 147, 781*
Dumont, M.: *860*
Dunning, R.W.: *258*
Dyck, D.: *385, 392, 393*

E

Eaton, J.W.: *413*
Ebanks, G.E.: *75*
Economic Council of Canada: *705*
Edmond, E.: *498*
Eichler, M.: *327, 328, 370, 371, 372, 452, 520, 638, 861, 862*

Elkin, F.: *259, 260, 329*
Ellen, M.: *592*
Ellis, D.: *50*
Epstein, N.B.: *625*
Ercul, D.: *639*
Erwin, A.J.: *330*
Eshleman, J.R.: *331*
Evans, P.: *377, 829, 876*

F

Fast, J.: *832, 934*
Fast, J.E.: *316*
Fedy, K.J.: *49*
Fels, L.: *91, 640*
Ferguson, R.: *65*
Fineman, M.L.: *185*
Finnie, R.: *206*
Fletcher, S.: *804, 805*
Foot, D.K.: *38*
Foote, C.: *568*
Foote, C.E.: *569, 582*
Forbes, W.F.: *908*
Foreign Service Community Association: *627*
Forman, J.: *300*
Fortin, G.: *234*
Foulché-Delbosc, I.: *482*
Fournier, B.A.: *629*
Fox, B.: *453, 454*
Fox, B.J.: *373, 455*
Frederick, J.: *934*
Frederick, J.A: *316*
Freeman, D.S.: *378*
Freeman, S.: *725*
Frideres, J: *534, 602*
Friendly, M.: *66*
Frizzell, A.: *916*
Frosst, S.: *207*

G

Gaffield, C.: *332, 483, 484*
Gagan, D.: *485, 486, 487*
Gairdner, W.: *333*
Galaway, B.: *642*
Gallaway, R.: *189*
Garber, R.: *4*

Garigue, P.: *424, 425, 426, 427, 428*
Gauthier, P.: *783*
Gavaki, E.: *261*
Gay Fathers of Toronto: *443*
Gee, E.M.: *129, 488, 489, 758, 784, 785, 830*
Gee, E.M.T.: *592*
Geller, G.: *440*
Gerin, L.: *429*
Gfellner, B.M.: *262*
Giblon, S.T.: *700*
Gibson, N.: *681*
Gilbert, R.: *534*
Girling, Z.: *640*
Gladstone, J.W.: *460*
Globerman, J.: *317, 318*
Glossop, R.: *374, 593, 909*
Goelman, H.: *69, 72, 935*
Goldenberg, N.: *639*
Goldstein, J.: *534, 535*
Goltz, J.W.: *340, 594*
Gonzalve, P.: *430*
Gossage, P.: *473*
Gottlieb, A.: *440*
Gower, E.: *334*
Grace, M.: *319*
Green, D.: *186*
Greene, B.: *51*
Greenglass, E.R.: *456*
Greenwood, L: *44*
Gregorovich, A.: *21*
Grenier, M.K.: *61*
Grigel, F.: *95*
Grindstaff, C.E.: *414*
Grindstaff, C.F.: *75, 415, 416, 595*
Gross, J.: *803*
Gross, P.: *716*
Gross, W.: *444*
Guberman, I.: *683*
Guemple, L.: *263*
Guest, D.: *831*
Guldner, C.A.: *596*
Guyatt, D.E.: *641*

H

Hagey, J.: *786*
Hall, D.R.: *92*
Halli, S.S.: *93*
Hamm, B.: *893*
Hanson, K.: *334*
Harlton, S.: *832*
Harney, N.D.: *264*
Harrison, D.: *628*
Harrison, P.: *490*
Harvey, C.D.H.: *245*
Haviland, W.E.: *394*
Hawkins, L.: *208, 623*
Hawley, D. L.: *22*
Hays, H.: *487*
Health and Welfare Canada: *23, 682, 833*
Health Reports: *148, 149*
Heaton, T.B.: *536*
Hébert, J.: *52*
Heer, D.: *537*
Heer, D.M.: *538, 539*
Heinlein, L.: *811*
Heinlein, S.: *811*
Heinrich, A.: *265*
Hendrix, C.: *529*
Henripin, J.: *417*
Henry, F.: *266*
Hepworth, H.P.: *5*
Herbert, E.N.: *267*
Herman, D.: *445*
Herold, E.S.: *812*
Hildebrand, E.: *245*
Hobart, C.: *340, 597, 598, 712, 717, 718, 719, 720*
Hobart, C.W.: *53, 54, 55, 94, 95, 268, 269, 599, 813*
Horna, J.: *402*
Hornick, J.P.: *229, 560, 912*
Housewives in Training and Research: *521*
Houston, S.E.: *504*
Hubey, C.A., Jr.: *539*
Hubey, C.A.: *538*
Huddleston, R.J.: *208, 623*
Hudson, J.: *642*
Hudson, P.: *379*
Hurley, D.: *643*

I

Income Security Programs, Canada: *834*
Inglis, J.: *237*
Irving, H.: *181, 187, 188, 193, 194, 380, 570*
Ishwaran, K.: *108, 109, 110, 111, 112, 270, 271, 311*

J

Jackson, J.A: *908*
Jamieson, K.: *571*
Jansen, C.J.: *272*
Jean, D.: *431*
Johnson, K.L.: *878, 935*
Johnson, L.C.: *67, 835*
Jones, A.: *47, 491*
Jones, C.L.: *335*
Jones, M.: *787*
Juby, H.: *910*

K

Kalbach, W.: *150*
Kalbach, W.E.: *336, 540*
Kallen, E.: *273*
Kanter, J.K.: *411*
Karlinsky, J.B.: *256*
Katz, M.B.: *492*
Keating, N.: *319, 832, 934*
Keating, N.C.: *395*
Keefe, J.M.: *320*
Kerr, K.: *319*
Killoran, M.M.: *895*
Kimball, M.K.: *785*
Kingsmill, S.: *228, 754*
Kirk, H.: *6, 7*
Kitchen, B.: *836, 837*
Klodawsky, F.: *529*
Kohl, B.: *396, 397, 493*
Kolish, E.: *473*
Kome, P.: *522*
Koulack, D.: *216*
Krashinsky, M.: *68*
Kraus, A.S.: *908*
Kreller, D.G.: *913*
Krishan, D.: *506*
Krishnan, P.: *337, 721*
Kronby, M.C.: *572*

Krotki, K.J.: *337*
Krotki, K.K.: *940*
Kryiazis, N.: *788*
Kuch, L.: *341*
Kurian, G.: *600*
Kurokawa, M.: *274, 275*
Kuzel, P.: *721*
Kyle, I.: *71*

L

La Novara, P.: *151*
Labour Canada, Women's Bureau: *877, 896*
Labour Canada: *897*
Laliberté, L: *628*
Lam, L.: *276, 308*
Lambert, C.: *673*
Lambert, R.D.: *541*
Landau, B.: *195*
Landsberg, M.: *863*
Langford, J.S.: *573*
Langlois, R.J.: *8*
Lapierre-Adamczyk, E.: *940*
LaPrairie, C.P.: *563*
Larson, L.E.: *338, 339, 340, 542, 543, 594, 601*
Latowsky (Kallen), E.: *277*
Laurin, C.A.: *838*
Lavoie, Y.: *146*
Lawrence, F.: *393*
Le Bourdais, C.: *839*
Lebevre, M.: *24*
LeBourdais, C.: *910*
Légaré, J.: *418*
Lero, D.: *69*
Lero, D.S.: *70, 71, 72, 209, 644, 878, 935*
Lewis, C.: *278*
Li, P.S.: *279, 280*
Li, S.: *645*
Light, B.: *901*
Lightman, E.: *669*
Linden, W.: *585*
Lindsay, C.: *152, 153, 936*
Lipman, M.: *9*
Litkenhaus, R.: *315*
Little, M.: *670*
Loewen, R.K.: *494*

Looker, E.D.: *523*
Lupri, E.: *402, 403, 602*
Luxton, M.: *457, 524, 525*

M

Macdonald, J.G.: *667, 673*
MacDonald, S.A.: *755*
Macdonnell, S.: *671*
MacDougall, D.J.: *603*
Mackay, H.: *672*
Mackie, M.: *458*
MacLellan, M.E.: *898*
Macrae, A.: *743*
Madison, B.: *840*
Malcabe, T.: *210*
Mandell, D.: *404*
Mandell, N.: *459*
March, K.: *10*
Marcil-Gratton, N.: *632, 839*
Marcus, C.: *11*
Marr, W.: *495*
Marsh, James H.: *942*
Marshall, D.: *633*
Marshall, K.: *879, 880*
Marshall, V.: *789*
Marshall, V.W.: *407, 790*
Martin-Matthews, A.: *76, 686, 687*
Matthews, A.: *688, 689*
Matthews, M.: *763*
Matthews, R.: *76*
Matthews, S.H.: *763*
Matthiasson, J.S.: *281*
Maureen, M.: *646, 881*
Mayer, A.J.: *413*
Maykovich, M.K.: *282*
Mazikins, B.: *135*
Mazur, C.: *25*
McAlpine, D.D: *668*
McCall, M.L.: *229, 232*
McDaniel, S.A.: *375, 756, 792, 793, 791, 794, 830, 841, 842, 864, 865, 911*
McDonald, P.L.: *912*
McGhee, M.: *398*
McGuinness, D.: *156*
McIrvin, Abu-Laban S.: *283*
McKenzie, B.: *683*

McKie, C.: *96, 154*
McKie, D.C.: *496*
McLean, L.: *690*
McMaster University: *155*
McMullin, J.: *779*
McPherson, K.: *26*
McQuillan, K.: *130, 666*
McVey, W.W. Jr.: *612, 684*
McVey, W.W.: *150*
Medjuck, S.: *497*
Meiklejohn, P.: *341*
Mendes da Costa, D.: *574*
Menear, M.A.: *575*
Messinger, L.: *722, 723, 724, 725, 746*
Millar, W.J.: *423*
Miner, M.: *432*
Ministry of Community and Social Services: *12, 13*
Ministry of the Attorney General: *576, 577*
Mishra-Bouchez, T.: *498*
Mitchell, A.: *230*
Mitchell, B.: *757, 758, 770*
Mitchell, B.A.: *759*
Mitchinson, W.: *894, 911*
Mohr, J.W.: *578*
Momirov, J.: *907*
Montgomery, B.G.: *913*
Moore, E.G.: *156*
Moore, M.: *135, 647, 648, 649, 650, 651, 654*
Moreux, C.: *433, 434*
Morrison, J.: *914*
Morrison, K.: *726*
Morrison, R.J.: *231*
Morrison, T.R.: *499*
Morrison, W.: *624*
Morton, M.E.: *579*
Morton, S.: *500, 652*
Moscovitch, A.: *915*
Mossman, M.J.: *381*
Munro, B.: *542, 543*
Myers, H.D.: *913*

N

Nagata, J.: *284*
Nagnur, D.: *604*
Nagnur, D.N.: *122, 123*

Naidoo, J.C.: *285*
National Advisory Council on Aging: *795*
National Council of Welfare: *73, 706, 937, 943*
National Information Services Corporation: *120*
Naus, P.J.: *796*
Neice, D.C.: *587*
Nelson, E.D.: *899*
Nelson, F.: *446*
Nelson, G.: *405*
Nessner, K.: *47*
Nett, E.: *501, 605*
Nett, E.M.: *342, 343, 606, 797, 798*
Newman, F.: *56*
Neysmith, S.: *377*
Neysmith, S.M.: *382*
Ng, R.: *286*
Nicholson, J.: *916*
Noivo, E.: *287*
Norland, J.A.: *760*
Norris, D.: *749*
Norris, J.E.: *344*
Northcott, H.C.: *691, 799*
Novak, M.: *800*
Nuttall, S.: *69*

O

O'Brien, C.: *447*
Oderkirk, J.: *89, 231, 607*
Ontario Advisory Council on Women's Issues: *866*
Ontario Law Reform Commission: *580, 747*
Ornstein, M.: *479*
Orton, M.J.: *814, 815*
Osterreich, H.: *547*
Owram, D.: *39*

P

Page, G.: *624*
Paletta, A.: *548*
Palmer, S.E.: *608*
Paris, E.: *727*
Parr, J.: *502, 503*
Parsons, M.D.: *653*
Pask, E.D.: *232, 581*
Paterson, G.H.: *113*
Payne, B.J.: *806*

Pearson, L.: *189*
Pelletier, A.J.: *157*
Pence, A.: *65, 69*
Pence, A.R.: *72, 74, 935*
Pendrith, F.: *677*
Pepper, S.: *25*
Peron, Y.: *147*
Perrier, C.: *934*
Peter, K.: *288, 289*
Peters, J.: *211, 212, 290, 345, 821*
Peters, J.F.: *57, 213, 214, 728*
Petrie, A.: *900*
Piddington, R.: *549, 550, 551*
Pike, R.: *215*
Pillemer, K.: *916*
Pinch, F.C.: *629*
Pineo, P.: *552*
Pineo, P.C.: *553, 609*
Podnieks, E.: *916*
Pool, D.I.: *346, 816*
Pool, I.: *654*
Pool, J.S.: *816*
Posner, J.: *801*
Posterski, D.C.: *45*
Premier's Council in Support of Alberta Families: *347*
Prentice, A.: *504, 901*
Prentice, B.: *496*
Price, J.A.: *291*
Priest, G.: *135*
Proulx, J.: *216*
Proulx, M.: *526*
Pryor, E.T.: *750, 751, 752*
Pupo, N.: *875, 876, 902*

R

Radecki, H.: *292, 293, 294*
Rajulton, F.: *58, 129*
Ram, B.: *158, 159, 419*
Ramirez, J: *286*
Ramu, G.: *114*
Ramu, G.N.: *77, 78, 79, 115, 116, 348, 554, 610*
Rao, K.V.: *80, 81, 98*
Raphael, D.: *761, 762, 765, 766, 767, 768*
Rashid, A.: *295*
Ravaneka, Z.R.: *58*

Ravanera, Z.R: *129*
Rayside, D. : *448*
Redmond, W.: *14*
Reed, P.: *496*
Rempel, J.: *82, 780*
Rhyne, D.: *611*
Richard, M.A.: *296*
Richardson, C.J.: *196, 217*
Richmond, A.H.: *297*
Roberts, C.: *702*
Roberts, J.R.: *729*
Roberts, W.L.: *882*
Robertson, G.B.: *912*
Robertson, H.: *685*
Robinson, B.W.: *612, 684, 899*
Robinson, J.: *250*
Robson, B.: *218*
Rochon, A.: *157*
Rochon, M.: *843*
Rodgers, R.A.: *160*
Romaniuc, A.: *159, 161*
Rosenberg, H.: *525*
Rosenberg, L.: *544*
Rosenberg, M.W.: *156*
Rosenblatt, E.: *814, 815*
Rosenfeld, M.: *505*
Rosenthal, C.: *298, 789, 802*
Rosenthal, C.J.: *299, 406, 407, 555, 763*
Ross, D.: *707, 708*
Rothman, L.: *66*
Rowe, G.: *506*
Royal Commission on New Reproductive Technologies: *748*
Royal Commission on the Status of Women: *903*
Rubenstein, J.S.: *349*
Rutman, L.: *491*
Ryan, J.P.: *192*
Ryant, J.C.: *844*
Ryder, B.: *449*

S

Sabagh, G.: *420*
Sachdev, P.: *15*
Sacks, D.: *673*
Satterfield, M.T.: *583*
Saucier, J.F.: *42, 59*

Sauvé, R.: *233*
Sayer, L.: *50*
Schlesinger, B.: *16, 27, 28, 29, 30, 31, 32, 33, 190, 300, 350, 351, 352, 353, 354, 355, 356, 357, 401, 408, 409, 410, 461, 462, 613, 614, 630, 633, 639, 655, 656, 657, 658, 659, 660, 661, 662, 663, 669, 673, 674, 675, 692, 693, 694, 698, 699, 700, 701, 702, 709, 730, 731, 732, 733, 734, 735, 736, 737, 738, 739, 740, 741, 742, 743, 754, 761, 762, 764, 765, 766, 767, 768, 817, 818, 850, 851, 852, 853, 883, 904, 917, 918*
Schlesinger, R.: *32, 33, 356, 357, 462, 701, 853, 883, 916*
Schneider, M.S.: *450*
Schoenfeld, S.: *301, 302, 545*
Schwenger, C.W.: *803*
Scott, K.: *60*
Segall, A.: *535*
Sehl, M.: *624*
Sevér, A.: *219*
Shields, M.: *72*
Shillington, J.: *916*
Shorter, E.: *919*
Siddique, C.: *309*
Siddique, C.M.: *303*
Silver, C.: *89*
Simon Fraser University: *695*
Sleighholm, S.: *14*
Smith, D.: *891*
Smith, D.E.: *867, 868, 869, 884*
Smith, H.: *624*
Smith, M.J.: *383*
Smith, N.F.: *61*
Snell, J.: *507, 508, 509*
Snell, J.G.: *510*
Snider, E.: *556*
Sobol, M.: *2, 17*
Sobol, M.P.: *3*
Social Planning Council of Metropolitan Toronto: *845*
Social Sciences and Humanities Research Council: *928*
Sommer, R.: *44*
Spector, A.N.: *529*
Spence, A.: *34*
Spencer, J.: *929*
Stasiulis, D.: *887*
Statistics Canada: *162, 163, 164, 165, 166, 167, 168, 169, 170, 171, 172, 173, 174, 175, 176, 321, 938, 939*
Stelcner, M.: *788*
Stephenson, M.: *870*

Stewart, A.: *473*
Stoffman, D.: *38*
Stone, L.: *885*
Stone, L.L.: *804*
Stone, L.O.: *805*
Stone, S.D.: *451*
Stout, C.: *97*
Strain, L.: *806*
Strong-Boag, V.: *511, 512, 527, 846*
Stuart, S.: *228*
Stubos, G.: *306*
Sturino, F.: *304, 305*
Sutherland, N.: *513*
Synge, J.: *514*

T

Tastsoglou, E.: *306*
Tavuchis, N.: *79, 348*
Taylor-Herley, S.: *379*
Tepperman, L.: *117, 335, 421*
Termote, M.: *807*
The Canadian Journal of Sociology: *358*
Thiessen, V.: *523*
Thomas, G.: *307*
Thomlison, R.J.: *582*
Thompson Educational Publishing: *177*
Thompson, K.: *154*
Thompson-Guppy, A.: *726*
Thomson, F.D.: *157*
Thomson, W.: *207*
Thornley-Brown, A.: *250*
Timpson, J.: *920*
Tindale, J.A.: *344*
Todres, R.: *410, 663, 664, 822*
Tomes, N.: *83*
Toth, A.E.S.: *744*
Transition: *745, 808, 921*
Tremblay, M.: *234*
Tremblay, M.A.: *435*
Trocme, N.: *188*
Trovato, F.: *220, 615*
Troyer, W.: *221*
Trussell, J.: *98*
Turcotte, P.: *99*
Turner, F.J.: *384*

116

Turner, J.C.: *384*

U

Urquhart, M.C.: *515*
Usher, C.M.: *769*

V

Vachon, M.L.S.: *696*
Vanier Institute of the Family: *18, 359, 360, 361, 362, 363, 710, 922, 923*
Vayda, E.J.: *583*
Veevers, J.E.: *84, 85, 86, 87, 88, 118, 364, 365, 770*
Verdon, M.: *436*
Verma, R.: *308*
Vogl, R.: *560*

W

Wachtel, A.: *563*
Wadhera, S.: *422, 423*
Wakil, E.A.: *617*
Wakil, F.A.: *309*
Wakil, P.: *376*
Wakil, S.P.: *119, 309, 616, 617*
Walker, A.J.: *322*
Walker, J.L.: *399*
Walker, K.: *724, 725*
Walker, K.N.: *746*
Walker, L.S.: *399*
Wallace, J.E.: *229, 912*
Ward, P.: *516*
Wargon, S.: *366, 367, 665*
Wargon, S.T.: *62, 930*
Warren, S.: *319*
Watson, R.E.L.: *100*
Watt, D.: *924*
Webber, M.: *19*
Weinfeld, M.: *249*
Weir, L.: *447*
Wertenberger, D.: *319*
Wesley, W.A.: *625*
Westhues, A.: *1*
Wheeler, M.: *677*
White, J.M.: *101, 618, 626, 933, 924, 925*
Whitehurst, B.: *368*
Whitehurst, R.N.: *634, 635*
Wigdor, B.: *775*

Wilson, J.J.: *235*
Wilson, S.: *636*
Wilson, S.J.: *331, 335*
Wine, J.: *440*
Wister, A.V.: *759*
Witney, G.: *160*
Wolfson, L.H.: *584*
Woon, Y.F.: *310*
Wu, Z.: *102, 103, 697*
Wylie, B.J.: *369*

Y

Yeager, A.: *341*
Yelaja, S.A.: *847*
Young, M.M.: *311*
Younge, E.: *848*

Z

Zhao, J.Z.: *92*
Zimmer, Z.: *93*

WEBSITES RELATED TO CANADIAN FAMILIES

- **www.vifamily.ca** .... Vanier Institute of the Family

- **www.cfc-efc.ca** .... Child and Family Canada

- **www.canadianparents.com** .... Canada Parents on line

- **www.cfc-efc.freespace.net/familywork** .... Family Work Connections

- **www.statcan.ca** .... Statistics Canada

- **www.archives.ca** .... The National Archives of Canada

Currently ArchiviaNet contains more than 3.5 million descriptions of different types of documents. The Web site allows consultation of an immense virtual catalogue that includes film descriptions, videos, sound recordings, photographs, works of art, caricatures, manuscripts and government files. ArchiviaNet also contains one of the most imposing collections of on-line research tools allowing researchers to undertake and often even complete their research off-site or prepare for their visit to the Archives. The system makes research quicker and more efficient, whether on-site or off.

RESOURCES RELATED TO CANADIAN FAMILIES

Applied Research Branch, Human Resources Development Canada, 140 Promenade du Portage, Phase 4, 4th Floor, Hull, Quebec, K1A 8J9. Publishes *The Applied Research Bulletin* (free on request), which has summaries of Canadian studies, including those related to families. A list of available papers can be obtained from this source.

Canadian Social Trends is published four times a year. Every issue has some article(s) dealing with demographic trends related to Canadian families. Subscription rate $34/year. Order: Statistics Canada, Marketing Division Sales and Services, Ottawa, Ontario, K1A O6T.

Family Connections magazine is published four times per year by the B.C. Council for Families, #204 - 2590 Granville Street, Vancouver, BC, V6H 3H1. Subscriptions by membership: $35/year.

Transition, published quarterly by the Vanier Institute of the Family, 94 Centrepointe Drive, Nepean, Ontario, K2G 6B1. FAX (613) 228-8007. Subscription by membership: $30/year.

National Council of Welfare, 2nd Floor, 1010 Somerset Street West, Ottawa, Ontario, K1A OJ4. Regular reports on diverse topics including Poverty in Canada. All reports are free if you are on the mailing list.

Statistics Canada. *2001 Census Consultation Guide*. Catalogue #92-125GPE. Available free of charge. This guides provides information on recent demographic and socio-economic trends. It highlights issues for the 21st century. Statistics Canada, 3-B-4, Jean Talon Building, Tunney's Pasture, Ottawa, Ontario K1A OT6.